Death
of the
Schooner
INTEGRITY

Death
of the
Schooner
INTEGRITY

by
Frank Mulville

CHARLES RIVER BOOKS
Boston

Library of Congress Cataloging in Publication Data

Mulville, Frank, 1924-
  Death of the Schooner Integrity.

  Earlier ed. (c1979) published under title: Schooner Integrity.
  1. Integrity (Ship)   I. Title.
GV822.I57M84   1981   797.1′24   80-39525
ISBN 0-89182-032-9 (hb)
ISBN 0-89182-033-7 (pb)

Published by Charles River Books, Inc.

One Thompson Square, Charlestown, MA 02129

ISBN 0 89182 032 9 (hb)   ISBN 0 89182 033 7 (pb)

Library of Congress Card Number 80-39525

Printed in the United States of America

Drawings by Walter Kemsley

Maps and diagram by Roger Robinson

Acknowledgements

The author would like to acknowledge with gratitude the help given him by many who have become friends, some through correspondence and others personally, since he started his investigation into the affairs of the schooner *Integrity*. The editor of *Yachting Magazine* kindly sent copies of articles. Mr Norman Fortier of South Dartmouth, Mass. sent the photographs of *Integrity*, Geoffrey Innes sent extracts from his log book, some of which are reproduced, and Mrs Innes supplied the photograph of *Integrity* under tow of *Captain Cap*. Those of the schooner under tow of *Iskra* were taken by Heather Dunn. Capt Abram, the Marine Superintendent of the Splosna Plovba Line was also most helpful. Information was supplied readily by everyone the author approached for help and he would like to extend his cordial thanks. Without Waldo Howland's help the book could not have been written.

F.M.

CHAPTER I

Like every journey ours was coming to an end and we were only anxious to finish it off. Three of us had sailed from Bradwell right up the east coast of England, across the flattened head of Scotland and down through the incomparable beauty of the west. I had loved it, in some ways more than any other cruise I have made. I found myself entirely captivated by the haunting, tranquil beauty of the lochs and by the bold, stark grandeur of the Scottish coast. We had found people who had taken us at our face value as voyagers from another land and had opened their hearts. Now, satiated with the magic of isolation—sheltered havens indented far inland from the sullen ocean, the vivid sea and mountains all around us— we were homeward bound. We had crossed Scotland back from west to east through the Caledonian canal and now there lay between us and home only 500 miles of the North Sea.

It was all far away, both in time and in distance, from the Bahamas, from Turks Islands and from the *Integrity*. Yet in the past year and a half the *Integrity* had never passed out of my consciousness. The memory of her and the strange circumstances of my association with her had grown fainter as time passed, as happens with all memories, but had never died. The schooner never quite relinquished her hold on me—somewhere, not far beneath the surface was the feeling that I had not heard the last of her. She had a strange talent for turning up where she was least expected, not only for me but for others who had been concerned with her. It was almost as if she possessed a power of her own, as if in some uncanny way she was more than the sum total of the materials and workmanship that went into her construction. Even here in the remoteness of Scotland she was close at hand.

We came down through the last of the locks at Inverness and into the Muirtown basin, a long and ample stretch of water with only one set of locks and the main line railway bridge between it and the sea, or to be more precise the Firth of Inverness. I was wondering whether to go straight out and lie for the rest of the afternoon and the night outside the locks in Inverness itself, or whether to wait until morning.

One of my crew would catch the train home leaving the other to help me bring *Iskra* back to Bradwell and I wanted to tie up convenient to the station and convenient to shops so that we could stock up with stores for the five or six day passage. By chance we saw a boat we knew lying alongside and as we motored slowly past I shouted across, asking his advice. "Stay the night here," he said; "you'll be more comfortable than in the town. You can lock out with us in the morning." We thanked him and looked around for a berth. There were a few yachts, a couple of coasters, a big old schooner but no space alongside the quay. In the end we selected a large motor yacht, or to be generous a motor-sailer, and breasted alongside. We threw a rope which was taken and made fast by a tall American whom we took to be the owner. He wore a tiny cap with a long peak, a sword fisherman's cap in American parlance. "Come on board later on and have a drink," he said.

There was much to do. I had work to do on deck before venturing into the North Sea from the sheltered waters of the canal and the protected lochs of the west coast. As I worked

2

end-for-ending *Iskra's* throat halyard—we had carelessly allowed it to chafe against the gaff jaws—I glanced at the yacht alongside. She flew an American flag from a neat jackstaff set in the taffrail. She seemed to be constructed entirely of plastic and stainless steel. Her mainsail was rolled away inside the metal mast in some cunning fashion and could be broken out by pulling a small stainless steel ring like the top of a beer can. All her sails set in like manner so that she seemed to have no halyards and no sheets. Everything worked electrically or by some magic which was not apparent. *Iskra* looked incongruous and slightly out of place alongside her. It was recognisable that they came from the same family but *Iskra* seemed poor and humble—covered with old fashioned rope, all made of wood, painted with paint, her big varnished tiller sticking out in primitive fashion from her rudder head and her long, archaic bowsprit. I reflected that I would rather be caught on a lee shore in a gale with the engine broken down in the old gaff cutter than in this shining thing alongside. She was a sort of picnic lunch party boat.

We took on stores and by the time everything was stowed and all the jobs were done it was late. The cruise round Scotland had been marred by foul weather, a soaking and a fright in the Pentland Firth and the rigours of wet and cold. The beauty of the place, the wild flowers, the birds, the tranquillity had made amends but we would all be pleased to get back to our homes. As we walked ashore in the evening, across the American yacht, the tall man bobbed up from a hatchway. "Why, you were going to join us for a drink," he said; "come right on board." He took us firmly round the decks and showed us the strange devices which drove this, to me, strange vessel. I suppose I am old-fashioned and behind the times—I am accused of being a purist, but this is not so. I will use anything, however modern, provided it is worth its space. Why—*Iskra* has electric light and an electric pump. The wheelhouse of this yacht was a marvel—I felt like a child on an outing to the Science Museum. Dials and levers and switches and flickering needles and coloured lights and automatic signals—there was even a wheel, although it was never used at sea, he said. I was relieved to get below into the saloon.

The tall man was the owner. We met his wife and two other Americans, an elderly, thoughtful-looking man and his wife. We were introduced in the usual way and in the usual way, being English, we forgot all the names immediately. The owner, on the other hand, fixed our names firmly in his mind and then, to make sure, wrote them down on a slip of paper to be incorporated later in the ship's log. This preoccupation with people's names is an interesting habit, peculiar, I believe, to the Americans. Perhaps it stems from a feeling of insecurity—the desire not to be caught at a disadvantage, to be sure exactly who you are dealing with. Or perhaps names mean a lot because they indicate racial origins. I admire the trait—it shows concern. We seldom bother about people's names until we have decided whether we are going to accept them as friends and equals—a form of casual arrogance.

The yacht was being taken to Norway. They had come across the Atlantic from somewhere on the eastern seaboard—I think it was in Massachusetts. She would be left in Norway until next summer and then the owner would come over and spend a few weeks in the Baltic. She had a paid crew on board and two Gardner diesel engines. I gathered the owner was a very experienced sailor who had owned many yachts and weathered many adventures. As I remember it the conversation was of no particular interest. The three of us were keen about our dinner and would happily have gone straight ashore. The owner was almost apologetic about his boat, explaining that in his advancing years he needed something that he could handle easily, that was reliable and safe and that he and his wife could manage by themselves. It was clear that he had gone to enormous expense to achieve this aim and to achieve a high degree of convenience and comfort below decks. The older American was a short, stocky man who had carried his good looks into his advancing years. He had soft, intelligent grey eyes full of imagination

4

and a slow, deliberate way of talking which suggested that every word was carefully weighed and considered. His wife, Katy, was small and very alive—like a bird. He showed great interest in *Iskra*. He had watched her come into the basin, had observed her lines and her gaff rig which he admired. "Sure looks a tough sea boat," he said. And then the tall American said, "I guess, Waldo, that's just the kind of little boat you admire."

For some minutes I had been experiencing an odd feeling about the older American. It was as if I had seen him before, had met him in the past or in some way knew him or knew about him. It is a feeling I have experienced a number of times in my life about people, or about circumstances or about what someone is going to say or do next—a sort of intuitive feeling. It has happened to me sufficiently often for me to know without doubt that the feeling, or impulse, or foreknowledge or whatever it happens to be is infallibly correct. Now I had this feeling most strongly about Waldo and for a moment or so I cast about in my mind trying to locate the true significance of it. And then suddenly it slotted into place, like the correct combination of a lock, and I knew without doubt who Waldo was and how I knew about him.

I said, "You're Waldo Howland?" He looked at me, surprised at my tone of voice. "From Dartmouth, Massachusetts?"

"That's right."

"You are the owner of the Concordia boatyard?"

"Why sure but. . ."

"You built the schooner *Integrity*—is that right?"

"Why yes I did—but how do you know all this?"

He and his wife both looked at me in astonishment. This was a hardly credible coincidence—a freak twist of chance that had landed Waldo and me beside each other in the cabin of this unlikely vessel. I knew Waldo and had known him for over a year although he did not know me and had never heard of me. I knew that he could have no knowledge of the story that I would have to tell him although that story concerned

5

him intimately. I knew that he would want to hear that story and I knew that only I could tell it to him. What unlikely hand had caught together these threads so that the three of us could meet—the ghost of the *Integrity* from across the ocean in Turks Islands, myself who had been witness to her last hours and Waldo who was her creator, who had loved her and who had shared in her glory? To Waldo and me at that moment nothing existed except ourselves, each of us bearing in his mind his own image of the schooner *Integrity*. Those images were far removed in their likenesses. To Waldo the *Integrity* was the noble schooner of his dream—the ship he had striven for over half a lifetime, planning and scheming and figuring her lines and her form and creating out of his own mind her specific identity. To me the *Integrity* was no more than a ruin, a wreck, a hulk—even a macabre joke. Yet I knew that the distorted picture of the *Integrity* that circumstances had thrust before me was incomplete. On my image also, Waldo's dream had always been present—a vague and shimmering shadow seen through the schooner's degradation.

There was silence for a few moments. Waldo was looking at me intently—his forehead wrinkled, his old seaman's eyes full of enquiry.

"Waldo, do you really know what happened to the *Integrity*?"

"Why—I guess so", his voice was steady but it betrayed a trace of emotion. "She was taken to Turks and there was a legal squabble and, well, I guess she's still there." I looked from one to the other, at Katy and him, striving to gauge the depth of their feelings. I had the impression that in some way I was intruding on a part of their privacy—that I had disturbed a subject that had been purposely laid on one side and purposely put out of mind. A boat is a strange thing. Inanimate—wood, iron, copper, canvas, rope, linseed oil, tar—maybe, but it all adds up to something more—something that can get inside a man's soul and carve out a place for itself that can never be forgotten. Once a boat gets inside it makes a man bigger, stronger, more complete. I knew that the *Integrity* had

To Waldo.... the noble schooner of his dream....

.... to me .... a ruin.

done this for Waldo—knew it from the schooner herself and knew it from him. I felt that Waldo and Katy were almost resentful that I should have knowledge about the *Integrity* that they had not. I needed to make some gesture, bring forward some evidence of my good will.

I made an excuse, left the cabin and ran back on board *Iskra*. It had happened again—another in a long chain of coincidences. The more I found out about the *Integrity*, not by any specific enquiry but through casual words dropped or odd meetings, the more I was coming to understand that my own experience and hers were strangely related. It had often crossed my mind that I should pursue this affair more deeply— I had often thought of discovering Waldo's whereabouts and writing to him. Perhaps he would tell me more about the schooner and perhaps he would be pleased to know the story of my own association with her. Now the good intention had been forestalled by this astonishing meeting. I went into *Iskra's* fo'c'sle ran my hand along the shelf under the bench on the starboard side and brought out my bo'sun's box. I had made the box to while away time in the Atlantic shortly before I first met the *Integrity*. I knew that what I wanted was in it.

I ran back on board the American yacht as quickly as I could and climbed down the ladder into the saloon. They were still sitting round the table as I had left them—the look of surprise and puzzlement was still present on Waldo's face. I put the box down on the polished table and began to empty out its contents. They made a strangely incongruous collection among this wilderness of plastic—sailmaker's palm, beeswax, needles, serving mallet, twine, a bottle of linseed oil, an old pair of scissors, a fid—all things indispensable to *Iskra's* daily running but which, I imagined, could find no possible use on board this modern and miraculous vessel. At the bottom of the box I came to what I was looking for. It was a large and beautifully turned nut with hexagonal sides, a wide flange and a rounded top—it was made of brass or phosphor bronze. I saw Waldo catch his breath and Katy let

8

out a little cry. They looked at each other across the table and Waldo said, slowly, "Why that's from the *Integrity's* wheel—the boss that fastened the wheel to the shaft—how did you get that?" I told him briefly how I had come across it—how I had put my hand on it where it lay on a broken shelf in the *Integrity's* worm-eaten and foul-smelling cabin—the same cabin that had been a home and a haven to Waldo for years. I had slipped the boss casually into my pocket and later it had found its way into *Iskra's* bo'sun's box where it had rested, forgotten until this moment. "I'll give it to you," I said to Katy Howland. "If there is any person who ought to have it—that person must be you." They were both silent.

It was through this chance meeting that the two contrasting streams of the *Integrity's* story were brought together in my mind. I had picked up snatches of information about her, I had heard stories about her all over the Bahamas, even in England. Before I met Waldo I had never measured my impressions of the schooner against an authentic picture. Waldo told me about her—described her to me as the one who had been most intimately concerned with her. He told me all that I could think to ask him and in turn I told him about the *Integrity's* macabre ending. There had been rumour and counter-rumour, conjecture, invention and inspired romance all up and down the Eastern Seaboard, where she had been famous, but no one knew the truth. I was the only person who knew the truth about the schooner *Integrity*.

CHAPTER II

I don't believe I know the real reason that made me leave England in the Autumn of 1974 alone in *Iskra,* bound for the Bahamas. I thought up a variety of excuses at the time, invented several more or less plausible rationalisations good enough for the consumption of my friends. I had already made one single-handed voyage across the Atlantic in *Iskra*— why another? Certainly the *Integrity* had nothing to do with it because at that time her name meant nothing to me. I must have been suffering from some deep seated unrest, some inner disturbance which demanded the calm, healing comfort of solitude. I had tasted solitude—it is a drug which takes hold of you and makes you want more of it. The reason I gave to myself satisfied neither myself nor anyone else. I was going to Nassau to see Tamarind on her birthday.

The Bahamas are a strange land, if you could call them land—nearly six hundred miles from Turks in the extreme south east to Grand Bahama in the north west. There are, perhaps, a thousand islands most of them uninhabited, some no more than coral reefs with a few wild palms waving their feathered heads. None of them measure more than a few miles across. The Bahamians, if you can find them from among the tourists and expatriates, are a most charming people—soft spoken with a lilting cadence to their voices which distinguishes them from the West Indians of the Caribbean. They are full of fun, full of music, ready to laugh and they consider themselves the equals of anyone.

If I had known then how difficult and harassing are the Bahamian out-islands for a man sailing by himself, I believe I would have approached Nassau from the east through the Providence Channel rather than up through the Exumas from the south. If I had done this, I would never have met Bill or the *Integrity*. At least two pairs of eyes are needed, two pairs of hands and two brains. There is nothing to get hold of. The land is all long, low, sandy strips of islands, shimmering with refraction, hiding themselves with protective colouring in an ill-defined and shadowy line along the horizon. It is often impossible to distinguish any mark or any feature; there are few trees and few buildings—one island can look identical with the next. At night, the secondary lights are of weak power and are often out of service. Although the weather, even in winter, is uniformly pleasant with a fresh trade wind to cool the hot sun, it is capable of sudden explosions when the wind swings to the north without warning and blows with a brief and bitter anger.

Then there are the coral reefs. They skirt every piece of land and they can be found in isolated patches far away from the land, often unmarked. Sometimes they are submerged a few feet below the surface and sometimes they are a line of vicious teeth, the ocean swell beating against them with a monotonous and always threatening roar. Inside the reef all is tranquil, the rumble somehow muted and benign because we are within its favour. From outside, the reef is a malignant and frightening barrier between us and peace.

The cuts or passages are often hard to identify. Sometimes, on the merest suggestion of leading marks, you have to take your heart in your mouth and sail helter skelter straight towards the reef, towards the certainty of destruction if you are wrong, with only the loosely held belief that the cut is really there. At the last minute, when disaster seems inevitable

12

and when it is too late to turn back, you will see smooth water and fly gratefully through into another world. You need, not a man by himself but one man aloft, another to spot the marks and a third to sail the boat. I have never been more frightened than when I took *Iskra* through the cut at Highburn Cay to the north of Turks Islands. It was blowing Force 7, the seas and the swell were enormous and there was no other place to go if I missed the passage. I hove-to for half an hour not more than a few yards from the reef, studying the Bahamian Guide. I still wasn't sure when I let the sails draw and put *Iskra* to it. Always, even with familiarity, the reefs and the cuts are a frightening experience.

I first met Bill in Puerto Plata, a small port in the Republic of Santo Domingo which occupies the eastern half of the island of Hispaniola with Haiti to the west. It is a convenient port of call for any yacht on passage between the West Indies and the Bahamas or the United States although for some reason it is little used by yachts. Perhaps this is because the Dominican Republic is Spanish speaking—the bureaucracy of entering and leaving the port can be tedious. The place has something of a reputation for lawlessness and vice although I have never found either to be irksome. I like it because it is full of vitality and the opposite extremes of happiness and sadness which are a part of the Spanish culture—a culture which seems to thrive in the environment of the Caribbean. The Spanish islands—Puerto Rico, Hispaniola and Cuba, to me have always been the most sympathetic. I was told about Puerto Plata by Captain Brown of the schooner *Freelance* in Antigua. "It's primitive," he had said, "but you can get all you want cheaper than anywhere else I know." I have been there three times.

I arrived off Puerto Plata at dawn on Christmas Day. I had the lights of the town in view for a few hours, slowly becoming clearer as I approached and then slowly dying away as the daylight spread over the land. The bulk of Mount Isabella behind the town materialised out of the night and turned to vivid green as the first rays of sunlight caught its

13

florescent, tropic lushness. The old Spanish fort at the harbour entrance hailed the day with a cracked and dissonant bugle call as the limp flag of the Republic of Santo Domingo was hauled lazily to the truck. An old man was fishing from a boat drifting in wide circles across the harbour entrance. The breeze that had brought me bravely along the coast had died to the merest air. The old man glanced up as *Iskra* approached. I saw him look and look again and then as I passed close to him I saw an expression of intense wonder and astonishment cross his features like a gossamer cloud across the sun. I could sense his feeling. "Madre de Dios—a man from the sea—alone in a boat—on Christmas Day—Madre de Dios", and he crossed himself gravely.

In the season of the sugar harvest Puerto Plata must be a hive of a place with ships in and out and a bustle of activity along the rickety wooden quays. In winter it is deserted. I saw a trimaran at anchor lying stern-to the quay with a rope ashore aft. There was a young man sitting on the foredeck—he seemed to be looking at *Iskra* as we came in, dropped anchor and swung round alongside. I thought he would jump ashore to take my stern line but he didn't move. As she swung, without a line ashore, she took too wide a sheer and the end of her bowsprit went between the trimaran's deck stanchions. The young man made no move to fend her off and no move when he saw the end of *Iskra's* bowsprit advance to within a foot of his face. *Iskra* swung a little more and there was a tearing, rending, splintering noise as two of the stanchions sprung off the deck—a shower of screws and little pieces of wood and plastic and a twang like a guitar string as the guard rail broke. People tumbled out of all the hulls. It was then that I saw Bill for the first time. He jumped ashore from the trimaran's stern, took my line and slipped it over a bollard. The young man was still sitting on the foredeck. After the shouting died down I asked Bill, "Why didn't he fend off?" "Oh that's Art," Bill said; "he's doing his T.M. It sure makes him calm."

I was sorry to have broken the trimaran's stanchions. *Iskra* doesn't like these animals and has to be led past them. She'll do them a mischief if she gets half a chance. Bill and I helped the man repair his boat and helped him mend a sail he had split. He was a quiet, pleasant American with his wife and Art who was his son. They had bought the boat in Puerto Rico and were trying to sail her back to the U.S. but they had no experience and weren't doing very well. They had read about sailing in a book and had started straight off. Bill was a visitor on board—he had nowhere else to stay. It sometimes isn't easy to avoid accidents when you are alone. *Iskra* is a big, heavy, ten-ton gaff cutter with a twelve foot bowsprit and sometimes she takes a bit of controlling. It's not too difficult at sea where there is usually plenty of room and plenty of time but sometimes in a harbour or an anchorage if she takes it into her head to be perverse, it's more than I can do to stop her. Her virtues outweigh her slightly unpredictable capriciousness—a sort of skittish desire to show her individuality. She is not a boat you can ever allow yourself to be complacent about—I believe she likes me to be aware of her femininity. I have watched her brooding at her anchor, cooking up mischief and hatching evil stratagems far too often to have any illusions about her. But her virtues are paramount. She is as steady as a rock in a seaway, she will sail out of trouble, she is sea-kindly and safe. If you ask her she will always give of her best.

Bill was a lanky, loose-limbed American from the South. He spoke slowly with a rich, deep drawl and he badly wanted a ride to Turks Islands from Puerto Plata. The distance is not great—less than a hundred miles—but there is no way of making the journey except by thumbing a lift on a yacht or a trading vessel. By plane you would have to go first to the U.S., then to Nassau and then to Turks—a journey that would cost more money than Bill had to spare. I had no wish to go to Turks—I had no business there, it was out of my way, it was remote and it would mean another and unnecessary customs and immigration clearance. Besides, I didn't know Bill—he might be an undesirable or an unwelcome person in

15

Turks for one reason or another in which case I knew the authorities would hold me responsible for him and make me pay for shipping him out again. I knew people who had been caught in this way in the Caribbean. "Sorry Bill," I said, "It's not on my way."

Bill was a man with whom it was easy to make friends. He folded his long body into *Iskra's* cockpit on that Christmas morning in the hot sun and in his slow, southern drawl he told me about Turks Islands, about himself and about the *Integrity*. Bill knew very little about the *Integrity's* origins—he had only heard of Waldo Howland by casual reference. He knew that she had been a famous yacht, built regardless of expense somewhere in Massachusetts, a copy of an old Baltimore schooner, or a trading schooner of the 1880's. He knew that she had been wrecked by a storm in the Atlantic, that her crew had been taken off and that, much later, she had been found adrift in the Atlantic and towed in to Turks Islands by an English yacht. The first he saw of her she was on the bottom in twelve feet of water not a hundred yards from the jetty of his newly acquired boatyard business in Turks Islands. It was after she was bought by Ron Bamber, where she lay on the bottom, that Bill became involved with her. He was employed by Bamber, I do not know on what terms, to raise her. The story seemed vague and confused and full of inconsistencies but it had a certain fascination because of the strangely varied personalities that were involved in it and because of the spell which seemed to have been cast by the schooner herself on all those who had to do with her.

I think perhaps I would not have been interested in the *Integrity* except that, by chance, I had been in a ship called by the same name. She was an ocean tug, a most charming and attractive little vessel and I became very fond of her. I had been her First Lieutenant—I think perhaps she was my first real responsibility and therefore she taught me thoroughly.

Bill and I went ashore in the evening and sampled the joys of Puerto Plata, which were diverse and plentiful, until far

16

into the night. We ended, rather drunk, sitting at a little iron table outside the cafe in the main square. A sleepy, unshaven waiter with a dirty napkin over his arm served us sweet

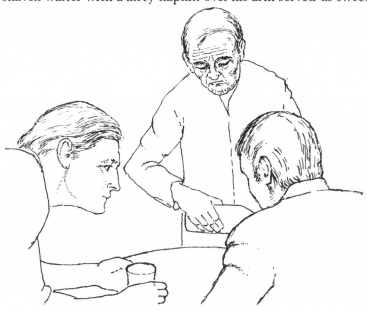

A sleepy unshaven waiter served us sweet
Dominican rum.

Dominican rum in short, stubby glasses, a cool breeze filtered through the cypresses in the plaza rattling their brittle branches, a pair of beggars, drunk and humiliated by poverty quarrelled on the steps of the cathedral, a girl and her novio hurried hand in hand towards some secret and auspicious destination. "Jeez, man—you sure should come up to Turks," Bill said with slurred and tipsy earnestness. "Why, goddam—it's the British Empire—I guess you guys don't have that much Empire left—it might not be there next time you come by." I looked at his grey eyes which had a touch of softness in them, his deeply grooved face, his long sensitive fingers. Maybe I could go to Turks without too much trouble and inconvenience—after all it wasn't far out of the way—it might be interesting—I wouldn't mind having a look at this schooner—I wouldn't mind getting to know Bill better, there was something essentially appealing about him. "Alright Bill—we'll start tomorrow."

CHAPTER III

I found that Bill knew Puerto Plata as well by day as by night. He took me off into the town the next morning and we stocked the ship. His Spanish was no more than fragmentary yet he seemed to know everyone, seemed to have a knack of getting what he wanted. Bill had been engaged in some commercial fishing venture between Turks and Puerto Plata—it had come to grief when he had quarrelled with his partner and he had found himself on the beach the wrong end with nowhere to stay and no means of getting back to Turks and his one-man boatyard business. For the past week or so he had been living on board the trimaran waiting for something to turn up—someone like me to give him a lift to Turks. The trimaran people may have been pleased to have him on board—his easy confidence was a source of strength to them in their unfamiliar adventure. Bill said we should buy as much in the way of fresh food as we could keep from going bad because the out-islands in the south of the Bahamas are barren—everything to eat except conch and coconuts is imported and very expensive. If he had been given his way he would have loaded *Iskra* so full of produce that there would have been no room for us below. "Man—we could clean up in Turks with this stuff," he said, "it's worth a small fortune." If he had been given his way he would have filled the bilges with contraband rum but I was against it and he accepted my restraint with a good grace. Smuggling and dubious business deals are not part of my stock-in-trade—I have seen too many people fall foul of the authorities. A small sailing boat is an ideal vehicle for such adventures but at the same time highly vulnerable—if you lose her you lose all.

It was evening before we were ready to go—the customs man had been. He had given us several forms and certificates in return for a carton of cigarettes, a glass of rum and a considerable bribe. I got *Iskra* ready for sea and asked Bill to stow his gear and the varied merchandise he had bought. "She'll move a bit," I said; "the wind's fresh." I reefed the mainsail, put on a small jib and we left the quay under engine with the last of the daylight. I stowed ropes and fenders and put up the mainsail while we were still within the shelter of the harbour. Outside, where it would be rough, all these jobs would take three times as long. Then I turned off the engine, set staysail and jib and put *Iskra* to the harbour entrance. As soon as she drew clear of the Spanish fort and the harbour mole she felt the strength of the wind and the size of the seas. The trade was blowing strongly, Force 6 or 7, we had it just abaft the beam. When she felt it she shot off like a grey-hound out of a trap—leaping across the seas, throwing spray over herself and revelling in the sheer fun of it as if she had been cooped up in harbour for a month instead of for a few days.

As *Iskra* gained distance from the shore the seas grew more even and she settled down to her usual steady gait. I was able to rig the self-steering and go below. I looked round the horizon but there was nothing to be seen except the diminishing shadow of Mount Isabella behind. It was a fine night, the waning moon gave outline to the waves and brought *Iskra's* sails and rigging into dim relief against the stars. There was no need for navigation lights on this empty ocean. She was steady on course—all was as it should be. I lit the oil lamps

20

She shot off like a greyhound out of a trap.

in the cabin. By their soft light, as it always does, the cabin grew large—an ample, gracious place full of warm, homely comfort. The motion inside the cabin was vigorous but Bill's stomach was up to it. He had done a fair bit of sailing in small boats although a strong wind and a cross sea in the ocean was outside his experience. He was impressed with the gaff rig which he had never seen before—the simplicity of it and the driving power astonished him. "These old boat builders sure did know a thing or two," he said.

21

We talked all night as *Iskra* raced to the north with the trade wind on her quarter. We saw no ship, no light—the moon left us, the stars remained, enveloping us in their own mystery—*Iskra* rolled and swerved and climbed and dived, shouldering her way through the ocean with steady, even strides. As we talked our questioning penetrated our minds, discovering weaknesses in each other and in ourselves, uncovering hidden recesses, revealing feelings and emotions that neither of us had known about before. We ranged over war and life, morality, duty to ourselves and to others. It was the beginnings of friendship.

Iskra had run her distance from Puerto Plata by eleven the next morning but I could see no land. I was uneasy. From the chart I saw that the south eastern end of Grand Turk is a mass of reefs and tiny cays for nearly twenty miles. If I missed Sand Cay to the south, I might run into this foul ground. A man I had met in Tortola on the passage out had showed me a copy of *The Yachtsman's Guide to the Bahamas.* "Anyone who tries to sail through the Bahamas single-handed has to be crazy," he said. He looked at my Admiralty charts and shook his head sadly. "I guess you don't stand a chance", and he gave me the book. I showed the book to Bill who knew it well. "Yeah", he said, "it's a swell book but it's all wrong. All to hell about Turks anyway." I found out that Bill was right. I found that the book had to be treated with as much caution as the reefs. Bill saw the land first. For some time I couldn't see it, even with binoculars, but after staring where Bill pointed for a few minutes a thin sand strip flickering against the horizon slowly took a vague and insubstantial outline. It wasn't far away—not more than two miles. I judged it would be easy to run right up to it without knowing it was there. "If that's the best this place can do for a landfall, I don't think much of it." "You'll get used to it," Bill said. As the wind eased and swung round towards the south we passed between Sand Cay and Salt Cay and soon had Grand Turk Island on our starboard side. It was a low strip of sand with no hills, no trees except a few clumps of casuarina and no

22

visible habitation. We saw a huge aerial, like a tilted bowl pointing to the sky and gyrating slowly round and round. Bill said it was a satellite tracking station built and operated by the Americans. Soon we came to a meagre collection of buildings spread round a wooden pier which jutted out into the open ocean. This was Cockburn Town. "Not much of a haven if it blows," I remarked thoughtfully. "If it blows," Bill said, "you get the hell out of it." As we approached I saw that a couple of Haitian sloops lay at anchor and, incongruously, a large catamaran. There were no other vessels. Piloted by Bill I took *Iskra* in towards the shore and across the five fathom line. As we crossed abruptly into the shallower water the sea changed colour from a deep to a paler blue. I could see the coral bottom clearly. Gradually it shoaled to ten feet and then, when we were in-shore of the two sloops and abreast of the catamaran we let go the anchor. *Iskra* swung to a lazy current and brought up to her cable, rolling uncomfortably in the long, easy swell. The wind had died to a breath—the barometer was falling steadily. I blew up the rubber dinghy and Bill and I rowed ashore.

It was easy to see that Bill was on home ground as soon as we got ashore. He had been away for several weeks and was delighted to be back. We soon ran into his friends. Chauncey was in charge of the NASA tracking station. He and his wife Heather had seen *Iskra* arrive from the verandah of their house which overlooked the ocean. It was a Sunday afternoon and there was no-one about. The place was so small that I thought there could hardly be many people to be about. Bill found the Harbour Master in his house and arranged to clear customs on Monday morning. Then we went to the verandah of Chauncey's house and were given long, rum drinks with ice. Heather was a South African. She had a charming family of three small boys—she was vivacious and attractive with a lovely deep voice—the sympathy flowed out of her. "Make this your home as long as you're here," she said; "of course you'll have all your meals here." There was a young American living with them whose name was Paul, an

23

engineering student having a year off from university. He and Heather ran a tiny tropical fish business, supplying the American market with live specimens. They were both expert divers. Paul had never been sailing. "That's something I've always wanted to do," he said. It was a lovely thing to be in a real house again with a real family—something I had not tasted since I left England six months previously. Before dinner I sniffed the weather. Chauncey said, "Look's like a norther coming in. If it does we'll shift you round to Hawk's Nest. They often miss out Turks and come to nothing—don't worry, we'll look after you." I was reassured.

Dinner was a delightful meal—lobster in some delectable sauce created by Heather, beer, sweet Bahamian pineapple. Bill had slept a bit on the passage up from Puerto Plata but I had been anxious and awake. Now, under the influence of food and pleasant company I could hardly keep my eyes open. Through the genial mist of good living Bill and Chauncey's conversation came to me like echoes from some subterranean cavern. "This guy Bamber wants her towed up to Cat," Chauncey was saying; "he figures he can get her hauled out there and fix her up like she was. I guess he's crazy. Why, the Windjammer's buzzing with it—there's a guy come over from Miami by plane to quote for the tow." Bill said, "Tow the *Integrity* to Cat? Haul her out and make her like new? Hell man—that guy must have a load of dough." Heather looked at me, saw the fatigue on my face, put her hand on my arm and said, "Frank—why don't you turn in— there's a bed next door." I pulled myself together. "No— thanks Heather, but I'll go back on board. I don't like to leave the old girl." I walked the few yards to the jetty in the dim light. There were a few houses, like Chauncey's in a straggling row along the foreshore then the wooden dock warehouses by the jetty and beyond, what looked like Government buildings, the brick Cable and Wireless office with a mast outside and a two storey wooden building in colonial style which I took to be an hotel. I launched the dinghy and rowed on board. It was calm and overcast. I was tired—nearly all-in.

24

I tapped the barometer—it dropped very slightly. Then I lay down and was asleep immediately.

A heavy bump woke me, as if *Iskra* had grounded on a rock. I sat up and listened but heard nothing. I got up and switched on the echo sounder but there was the same 9 feet there had been before I went to sleep. It was almost light—I had a headache. I looked round the anchorage. *Iskra* had swung with an on-shore wind and was lying stern-to the jetty and about 200 yards off. The weather still looked ominous but not noticeably worse than when I went to bed. One of the Haitian sloops was recovering her anchor and hoisting a patched and ill-fitting sail. "It must have been imagination," I said to myself and went back to my bunk. In a few moments, when I was almost asleep again, there was another bump. It jarred the whole ship. "Christ—she's ashore." I jumped out of bed and immediately pressed the starter button. She must be grounding on a coral head—that was why it didn't show on the sounder. The engine started and began to tick very slowly. Then I pulled on a pair of trousers. In the next second there was a grinding, crushing, splintering noise followed by the familiar "twang" and at once I knew what had happened. I put my head through the hatch. Yes—dammit. I had left the engine in gear—careless. *Iskra* had started to move ahead and now she was gouging the catamaran with her bowsprit. She had already carried away a stanchion and had broken her own bobstay. Now the bowsprit was attacking the heel of the cat's mast—I could see the whole lot tumbling down in minutes. I put the engine into neutral but by now the bowsprit was wedged across the cat's deck and was beginning to do damage as the boats rolled in the swell. I jumped aboard the cat and tried to prize this lethal weapon away from the mast. At first it wouldn't come and then it did come with a rush and the two boats swung apart leaving me on the catamaran's deck. This was not a good day. Then I saw Bill and Chauncey on the jetty. They were shouting something and waving their arms wildly. The wind was beginning to freshen.

I looked helplessly at *Iskra* 30 feet away and then I

shrugged my shoulders, dived over like an idiot and swam back on board. By the time I got into the dinghy and rowed ashore, leaving *Iskra* and praying she wouldn't hit the coral again, the wind was getting up. Bill said, "What in God's name have you been doing?" and then Chauncey said, "We've got to get you out of this place quick." By now it was beginning to blow. It was all I could do to row the tiny dinghy back on board against the wind. *Iskra* was already pitching at her anchor, the broken bobstay hanging into the water from the bowsprit end. Both the Haitian sloops were off, making their way south towards the Hawks Nest anchorage. The Haitians are superb sailors and it is often wise to follow their lead. They carry no barometer, no sextant, no charts and often no compass and yet they navigate their broken-down old boats for hundreds of miles from Haiti up through the Bahamas chain, sometimes making long sea passages. The sloops are about *Iskra's* size, perhaps a little bigger—they have no engine, their sails are old, thin and ragged, their spars are often unfinished branches fastened with flimsy gear. The hulls are thrown together on some Haitian beach of unseasoned timber, leaky and run down. Yet they can be seen all over the Bahamas loaded to the gunwale with fresh provisions from lush Haiti. Each of them has made a long and difficult sea passage to get there. They told me that the rewards of the trade are high, as is the casualty rate.

Iskra's engine was still running when we got on board. Bill and I heaved the anchor home and Chauncey slammed her into gear. As she gathered her way I set the staysail and the reefed main. The wind was increasing fast. We covered the distance to the south end of Turks very quickly, passing the two sloops which seemed to be making heavy weather of it. From the end of the island a line of breakers stretched to the south for as far as the eye could see. "Where's the entrance Bill?" "Right there", and he pointed to a wall of white water which appeared to have no break in it. I was undecided. Left to myself I would have made for the open sea and ridden it out in comfort, returning when the weather moderated.

The norther was unlikely to last more than a day. On the other hand Bill and Chauncey seemed to know what they were doing. Bill, after all, had a boatyard in Hawk's Nest and should be familiar with the channel. Chauncey had the manner of someone who knows what he is about. "Alright," I said, "You take her in", and I tried to close my mind to the whole affair. We turned off the wind and Chauncey put *Iskra* at the reef. Bill climbed aloft with remarkable agility and stood on the cross trees. Chauncey was at the helm, I sat in the hatch biting my finger nails. *Iskra* began to race towards the reef with the wind behind her. I could see no marks, nothing to distinguish one pile-up of foam from the next. Bill shouted his instructions from aloft. "Starboard a bit—steady—starboard again." Now we were on the edge of a gybe, racing towards the reef, the slow rumble increasing in intensity. The water was changing colour as it shoaled—from blue to aquamarine to palest blue to green to pale green and finally to a colourless translucence when the bottom stands out in every detail and when it is time to pray or to turn round. I shut my eyes and prayed. The reef thundered. Then Bill shouted "To port Chauncey—we're there." *Iskra* swung round, heeled to the wind and shot ahead. In seconds the reef was behind us and we were weaving our way through a vivid and tranquil paradise of coral, still guided from aloft, the reef no more than a diminishing thunder behind us like traffic in a busy street.

I took the mainsail off as we picked our way through the twists and turns of the Hawk's Nest anchorage. Soon I could see the jumble of sheds and huts which was Bill's boatyard—then the spindly wooden jetty and then the *Integrity* swinging to a rope mooring. We dropped *Iskra's* anchor within a few yards of her. Chauncey and Bill went ashore—Bill to take Chauncey back to Cockburn Town on the back of an old motor cycle. "See you later," Chauncey said; "Heather says you've to come to dinner." For the first time in days I was alone and able to relax. I had something to eat, took a couple of aspirins, found a can of beer, rigged an awning over the cockpit and sat surveying the scene at Hawk's Nest anchorage. There was little to see or hear—no other person, only the gulls crying and the murmur of the reef, a sound which I was to learn is never far away in the Bahamas.

The *Integrity* lay silent, alone, friendless. It was a long time since any hand had shown her care and compassion. She swung to her lines in a spiritless fashion as if she no longer cared. She was at the end of her resources, she had struggled through it all and now she wanted no more of it—she was finished, done for, written off. The unmistakable signs of her good breeding, her class, her polish, only made her present plight the more pitiful—like an old, poor actor who has once entertained kings. She was a mockery of herself yet the lines of her sweet sheer were still there, the lift and flare of her bows, the rounded and graceful contours of her stern, the dignity of her gently curving forefoot—all cried out together that this was a cruel and tragic wastage of a thing of beauty.

In due time Bill came for me on the motor cycle and we rode back to Cockburn Town across the sandy track which wound its way through the arid and deserted salt pans which had once made the island prosperous. The salt trade was dead—killed by modern refrigeration. The economy of Turks Islands had never recovered. Over dinner, Chauncey and Bill and Heather talked about the *Integrity* because, yet again, she had become the consuming topic of conversation on the island, once again her name was on everyone's lips. I stayed the night in Heather's house—the norther had made only a brief disturbance in the settled pattern of trade wind weather and I knew that *Iskra* was safe in the Hawk's Nest.

The next day, belatedly, I cleared customs and immigration and then Bill took me back on the old motor cycle—its exhaust was clapped out but no one on Turks minded the noise. I was already anxious to be off on my way through the Bahamas to Nassau. It was getting near Tamarind's birthday although I still had time in hand. I would have to mend the broken bobstay and there were a couple of jobs to do before I moved on. Heather had persuaded me, I confess

28

with no difficulty, to share her hospitality for another day but then I must be gone. She and Paul had promised to take me diving on the reef and I knew it would be a rare experience. She told me she had discovered an underwater cavern, easy to enter even for an inexperienced diver, where the strange and beautiful world of the ocean's floor could be observed. It was a fine morning again. A soft, cool breeze mottled the surface of the anchorage with tiny wavelets, white clouds stacked themselves in strange and wonderful shapes—it was warm and blue and all was at peace. For a few minutes I sat on the end of Bill's jetty, dangling my legs and gazing idly at the two yachts side by side—the trim, sturdy figure of *Iskra* that I knew so well and loved so much and the dejected schooner, battered and scarred and misused. And

Dangling my legs and gazing idly at the two yachts side by side.

then, for no reason that I know of, an idea came to me. It brought a sort of excitement that flushed through my whole body—a quickening, an increased perception, a racing of the mind. "I wonder—I wonder if she could do it", and then I said to myself again, "She just might—she could if she tried—it's just possible", and then as the idea gained strength by its own momentum, "By Christ—I believe she could—I believe it's worth a try."

CHAPTER IV

There is in all of us who have had to do with boats or ships a suspended ambition which lives in the nether regions of the mind, to build a boat to our own design or, if not physically to build a boat, to cause a boat to be built. To build a schooner is a refinement—there is something romantic and appealing about a schooner, she has a dignity of her own, is a cut above average, in a special category, a class by herself. To build a boat is a fine thing but to build a schooner is of a different order. We approach the problem according to our limitations and profit from the result according to our natures. Don Ridler, whom I had met in Antigua on the passage out, built *Eric the Red* for £100 out of scraps of timber begged or borrowed from dumps. He was a proud and happy man. A Swede I came across in the Azores had just taken delivery of a new yacht which cost £100,000. He was miserable. When Waldo Howland set out to make reality of his ambition he had several clear advantages—he knew what he wanted, he was a man of means, he was the owner of a considerable boat-building business and he came from that part of the world where schooners were invented. The first fore-and-aft rigged two master schooner was launched at Gloucester, Massachusetts in 1713, only a handful of miles

31

from Waldo's home. The Gloucestermen, fishing and trading schooners and later the whalers of New Bedford, were common on the eastern seaboard of the United States for a hundred years and the rig spread all over the world. When Waldo built the *Integrity* he was reaching back through the experience of his family who had been concerned with boats and ships on the Massachusetts coast almost since the invention of America itself.

As it happened, Waldo had an old friend who was himself steeped in the sea lore of the coast. Captain Culler was a traditionalist who believed that the old and well-worn ways of building, maintaining and sailing boats which he had acquired through a lifetime's work, were still valuable and relevant to modern experience. He had worked up and down the coast since the turn of the century, knew how to use the adze, knew how to make a builders' model and lay off her lines. He was a skilled shipwright and a designer who had worked with the Concordia boatyard, Waldo's family business, many times before and had himself designed many fine boats, including schooners. In 1929 Captain Culler built a replica of Slocum's *Spray*. He had lived aboard her for seventeen years and had sailed her backwards and forwards to the Bahamas, chartering for a living where the weather was favourable. His mind worked in terms of Stockholm tar and pitch and linseed oil and tallow and kerosene and white lead and black asphalt stikkum. He believed that good boats were constructed by craftsmen who knew how to work good, honest, natural materials with good, simple tools—he was a craftsman himself and his blood ran salt. Captain Culler was just the man to build Waldo's schooner and the two of them put their heads together.

Captain Culler must have been vastly influenced by Slocum. The *Spray* herself had been built in 1892, or re-built it is more accurate to say, in Fairhaven, right alongside where the Concordia yard now is. What is now called Slocum River is the next creek to the west from the spot where the *Integrity* was built.

Captain Culler — he was a craftsman himself and his blood ran salt.

The influence of the *Spray* can be seen in the *Integrity's* lines and in her construction. *Integrity* had the same stern and the same bow—she had a more pronounced sheer than the *Spray* and a finer run aft. Looking at pictures of the two boats their likeness is remarkable but the *Spray* was more powerful in her after parts. The *Integrity* seemed to be all

33

bow—her stern trailed off ignominiously.

The *Integrity's* keel was laid in the autumn of 1961 and she was launched in December 1962. She may have been something of a fling—at least an indulgence. Waldo had owned and managed the Concordia yard for many years and under his careful, thoughtful supervision the business had prospered. The profits of the war years had been consolidated later by Waldo's flair for correctly interpreting modern trends in design. The yard built over a hundred well-proportioned, comfortable, safe and not too expensive yawls of about thirty feet waterline. They built nearly five thousand small day sailers—the Beetle Cat boats as they are called. Waldo told me that these paid for his bread and butter for many years. The Concordia yard has a parallel in England in the Littlehampton yard of David Hilliard which built *Iskra*. The same sound principles of boat building were married to the same shrewd appraisal of the market to give a like measure of solid, creditable success. There was nothing to do with bread and butter about the *Integrity*—she was built withour regard to expense. She was Waldo's crowning extravagance, the tangible fruits of a lifetime's good husbandry. He went to town on her.

Integrity was a gaff schooner of 30 tons. She measured 52 feet overall and 44 feet on the waterline, had a beam of 15 feet and a draft of 6 foot 9 inches. Her rig was nicely proportioned—the two masts were nearly equal in height, the main mast was no more than a foot or so longer but it carried a high top-mast so that she could set a big working topsail, which run up and down on hoops and could be brailed to the main mast head with the mainsail was furled. She had a bowsprit with a flying jib-boom and carried a big working staysail and an overlapping jib. The rig was designed with a smaller than usual mainsail and larger than usual foresail and headsails so that she was well balanced in spite of her long straight keel which could have made her heavy to steer. She carried a fisherman staysail between the masts. Waldo said that she would look after herself for hours on end without a hand on the wheel. Her sails had been specially made of tan-barked cotton duck canvas by Gowans of West Mersea, England. She must have been a lovely sight.

Reading between the lines of all that has been written about her and having regard to what Waldo himself told me, it is clear that her design sacrificed speed to windward and efficiency for the sake of tradition. She had the virtues of the old but she had the old's vices with them. She was heavy and slightly under-canvassed. She didn't like pointing to windward—had a tendency to sag off. It was a job to get her through stays in a strong wind and a rough sea without a touch of engine and, from the look of her, her stern must have been vulnerable in a heavy following sea. The dinghy, slung in davits across the stern would only add to this vulnerability. The place for a dinghy at sea is on deck, securely lashed, not hanging up in the wind. On the other hand she would sail fast and steadily off the wind with a restful, easy motion. She was sea-kindly. She suffered from the split personality of being a scaled-down version of a larger vessel—the original packet schooners of which she was in part at least a copy were all much bigger. There is something about the laws of scale which does not allow for a mathematical contraction. Always something is slightly odd, out of proportion, not quite as it should be. People standing on the *Integrity's* deck looked larger than life—the flying jib-booms and all the stays that go with them, an essential part of the rig of a larger vessel, looked pretentious because they were unnecessary. You can't fake a boat—she is what she is and if you try to make one sort or size of boat into another for reasons of sentiment, the result is often slightly absurd. Not that the *Integrity* was absurd—she was not. She was unusual, perhaps a little eccentric when set against a modern schooner of her size.

The *Integrity* had all the resources of the Concordia yard behind her. She had been in Waldo's mind for years and for years he had been scheming towards her—saving up timber, working out details, striving to transform his vision into practical terms. Her keel was laid in the open, on a piece of waste ground two miles from the Concordia yard—behind one of the sheds where the Beetle Cats are built. The land there slopes gently down to the sea half a mile to the south. Captain Culler made a model. When it was completed and its finer points gone into at length by the local salts and nautical wiseacres her lines were laid down on the loft floor and moulds were made. She was built of locally grown white oak which was used for the wood keel, the keelson, the frames and the planking up to the waterline. Above the waterline she was planked with hard pine which was taken from a demolished school building. Her decks were of locally grown white pine. Her rudder was made from a piece of specially imported greenheart—a heavy, strong wood which grows in the tropics and is said to be impervious to marine borers. Because she was to be a yacht and not a work schooner Captain Culler gave her a 25 foot long iron keel for strength and ballast. For inside ballast she carried stone paving blocks which fitted neatly between the frames. She was held together by 3 foot long 1½ inch diameter iron keel-bolts and she was fastened with iron spikes. By the time the snows came her frames and her deck beams were already up and the timber seasoned through the winter with the aid of Captain Culler's patent brews of linseed oil and kerosene. A gang of twelve men worked on her including two of Waldo's sons. They used traditional tools supplemented only by an electric planer, a bandsaw and electric drills. The waste ground rang with the subdued but purposeful sounds of craftsmen at work—plane, maul, chisel, cutting and hewing and rendering to size and shape the massive timbers. Captain Culler with his bowler hat, his thin-rimmed spectacles and his adze, at work on the deadwood could have passed for the old mariner himself. The spring and summer of 1962 saw her decks in place, her deck houses and hatches completed and the fancy turned stanchions and rail round her poop in position.

Below decks her accommodation was dominated by the engine room which together with tanks, CO_2 bottles, batteries, generator and space for tools and spares took prime space, the full width of the ship amidships—another disadvantage of scaling down from a larger vessel. The engine was where the packet boat's hold would have been. The shaft was driven through the centre of the ship and turned a 28 inch three-bladed propeller which must have caused enormous drag when under sail. The engine was a 100 h.p. Westerbeke diesel with a 3-to-1 reduction gear which gave the *Integrity* 7 knots cruising speed. If she was short on canvas she had plenty of diesel power. Abaft the engine was a nicely appointed owner's cabin with panelled bulkheads, comfortable berths, its own lavatory and its own bogey stove. A hatch gave on to the deck beside the wheel. This was Waldo's place—his home from home. Together with the engine, it accounted for nearly half the available space below. The main accommodation was for'ard through a passage on the starboard side of the engine room, past the stoutly made wooden box which contained the starter batteries. The main cabin, with another lavatory, four bunks, settees, a big swinging table amidships and various hanging lockers was immediately abaft the galley which had a big coal-fired stove, for cooking and to keep the accommodation warm. There was a refrigerator to starboard and a good sink and work-top opposite. The fo'c'sle had two more pipecots making eight berths in all and another lavatory. The ship was lined throughout, from the keelson to the beamshelf with pine tongue and groove. She was salted inside the lining between the ribs and frames—an old schooner dodge to discourage rot.

The main accommodation was workmanlike, comfortable and in good taste. She was a very pleasant ship to live on board. Expense had not been grudged yet there was nothing in her that was fussy or out of character. When the hull was completed and painted dark green the *Integrity* was a splendid sight. There can be few modern yachts either in America or in Europe that were built with such loving care, such attention to detail and of such carefully selected materials. On a frosty morning in December 1962 she was launched. The fence between the Concordia property and

37

Col. Green's estate was breached and she was carried sideways, with heavy slings round her, by two mobile cranes, to the road and then down to the wooden jetty inside Round Hill Point. She was lowered gently into the water—she rode the sea prettily.

Integrity was towed out round the Dumpling Rocks, outside White Rocks and Keel Rocks and past the Padanaram breakwater to the Concordia boatyard's dock near the bridge across Appanagansett Bay, to be masted and rigged. Two pines were found growing in Dartmouth and were cut, fashioned with adze and plane and stepped, suitably treated with Captain Culler's goo, to season through the winter. Her rigging was made up of galvanised wire, wormed, parcelled and served with small stuff and then tarred with Stockholm tar specially procured from England. Ironwork for chain plates and deck fittings was sent for from Nova Scotia. Rigging screws, or turnbuckles, were spurned in favour of dead-eyes and lanyards. An old ketch I once owned used this ancient system and I confess I prefer dead-eyes and lanyards to rigging screws for this type of vessel. But Waldo and Captain Culler had me beaten when it comes to purism. I used artificial fibre rope for lanyards—Waldo sent to England for four stranded Italian hemp which was first stretched and then treated with tar and beef tallow. All the *Integrity's* cordage was of natural fibre— a luxury I have never wished to allow myself when rigging old boats. Synthetic ropes are stronger for their size, pass more easily through the blocks, coil without kinking and do not stretch, shrink or swell. Manilla, which was used all over *Integrity,* is a difficult rope, particularly when wet, although in some respects it is pleasant to handle and is not so easily chafed. All artificial rope burns if it is allowed to run through the hands but I believe this is a small price to pay for its advantages. But I differ fundamentally with Waldo and Captain Culler. I will use any material or any modern device if I think it is better, Waldo and Captain Culler, I believe, revere the old for its own sake. As Slocum himself said, "To be a sailor you don't have to hang a tar bucket round your

38

neck."

The *Integrity's* steering gear was a copy of that used on the *Spray*—a wooden drum mounted on a saw-horse, several turns of rope passing through blocks on the tiller end and on each side of the ship. It is a simple method and was used by Slocum because it was cheap and he could make it himself. Waldo used cotton line soaked in hot tallow—he told me that one set of lines lasted seven years. But it was vulnerable compared with modern steering gear—ropes lying across the deck could be damaged. Her anchor windlass was mounted on a massive samson post, a 12 inch by 18 inch piece of oak. the anchors themselves Waldo had got from a fisherman who had dragged them up in his trawl. Her shrouds had wooden ladders up to the cross trees on both sides and on both masts, her side-decks gave a clear run from fo'c'sle head to the wheel, a handsome and artistic piece, cleverly inlaid with fine-grained black walnut. As a concession to the modern world the *Integrity* carried ship-to-shore radio.

Any fine ship can be criticised—every seaman has his own theories, his own prejudices, his own ways of thinking. A ship, after all, stands out for all to see and it is the prerogative of those who know, or think they know, to pull her to pieces and put her together again. It is done to every ship that sails and will always be done. I hope Waldo and Captain Culler will forgive me for my opinions. Whatever defects the *Integrity* may have had, she was by any reckoning, a magnificent vessel. Under Waldo's rule she was immaculate—deep green topsides, a gold line sweeping for'ard to emphasize her sheer, from her gold name-board to the elegant filigree round her clipper bow. The subdued effect of her dark hull and her tanned sails was nicely set off by a line of white traced along the length of her from the tip of her jib-boom through her capping to the stanchions and rail round her stern. Her decks were flush with no hatches or deck-houses or companion ways protruding upwards to spoil her line. She carried her canvas easily, the lay-out of her gear as handy and as trim as you would expect to find in a working vessel. A hundred years rolled back as she coasted down the Massachusetts shore, at one with the rhythm of the ocean swell. She was the *Integrity* and as Waldo had intended, her name condensed to a single word the essential quality of her.

Waldo owned her until 1970. She became a familiar sight on the east coast of the United States, cruising from Massachusetts Bay to the Chesapeake, around Cape Cod, into Long Island Sound and Delaware Bay. Everybody knew her, everybody in every yacht club up and down the coast had seen her or heard of her. Copies of her were built in fibreglass—in two sizes I believe—they are still popular on the coast. It was an event when she arrived in port. Waldo first took her to the West Indies in the autumn of 1967, setting off from the east coast, making a huge offing towards Bermuda and then sailing south with the wind on his port side. In Grenada he met Geoffrey Innes who was the owner of a converted Brixham trawler called *Captain Cap*—a vessel that Waldo much admired. Innes liked Waldo and thought a great deal of the *Integrity*. For a few years she was successfully chartered on the coast, always being carefully and wisely handled and never finding herself in more trouble than she could manage. In 1969 Waldo chartered the *Integrity* to an old friend, Col. Herrington, who took her across the Atlantic to the south of Ireland to the bicentenary celebrations of the Royal Cork yacht club and later in the same season to the Beaulieu River for a meeting of the Royal Cruising Club. By chance, a friend of mine was also in southern Ireland in 1969 and went on board the *Integrity* several times. He told me that the schooner was much admired but he also remarked on the same peculiarity that I had detected—that there seemed to be something odd about her proportions, some ambiguity in her design which was hard to pin down. She returned to the U.S. by way of Portugal and the trade wind route to the West Indies.

By now Waldo was retired—he believed he was getting old, his interests kept him fully occupied, he was a trustee of the marine museum at Mystic Seaport on the Connecticut coast. In 1970 he decided to swallow the anchor and to sell the

40

Integrity. He had conceived her, built her and sailed her faultlessly around the American coast and to the West Indies. He had proved that with proper handling and proper understanding she was a ship that would go anywhere in the world in

Waldo was a careful owner and considerate to his ship.

comfort and in perfect safety. Waldo was a careful owner and considerate to his ship. He did nothing spectacular with the *Integrity,* he simply sailed her as he knew she should be sailed. He told me he had never been out in her in what he considered really bad weather—perhaps it is the ships and their crews that make their own weather. One man's gale may be another's hurricane. At all events, under Waldo the *Integrity* never put a foot wrong. He could not have known it but when he sold her he signed away her life. As Captain Culler put it, "She was acquired by lubbers who ruined her."

The schooner *Integrity* — a fine vessel by any standards.

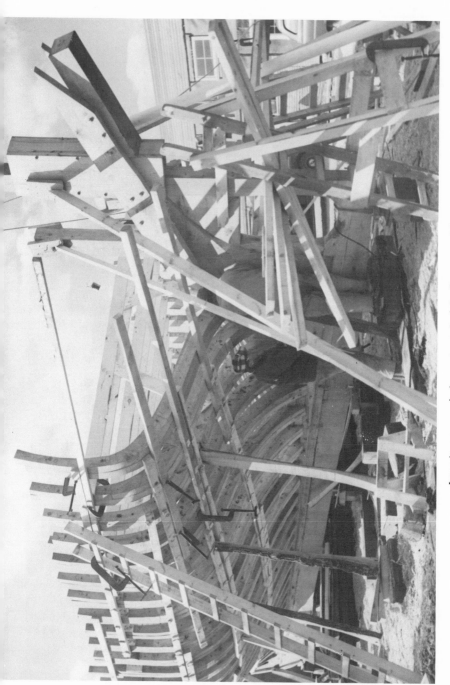

Integrity was massively constructed of the finest materials.

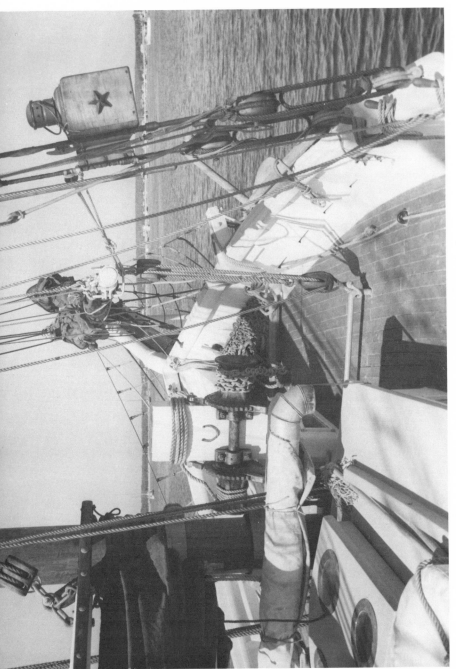

Integrity's gear — no concessions to modernity.

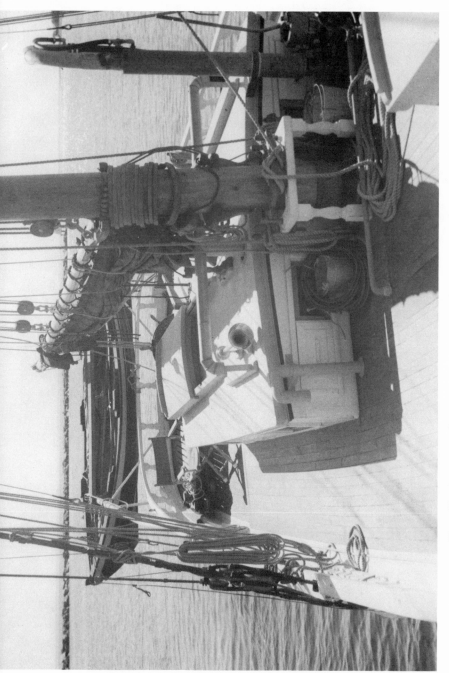

The pulling boat across *Integrity*'s stern — a source of danger in a heavy following sea.

CHAPTER V

"She was acquired by lubbers who ruined her." I believe that in his simple, sailor's way Captain Culler described what happened to the *Integrity* with devastating accuracy. Certainly if Waldo had known what was to be her fate he would never have sold her—the schooner meant too much to him, was too closely bound up with his own life. He had been living with her for years—if not with the schooner herself the thought of her, the conception of her had been a part of him for as long as he could remember. Like *Iskra,* the *Integrity* was something that had been created. She was not any man's plaything nor was she any man's easy way to a quick buck, a sharp deal, a slick proposition. There may be boats that can be used in this way—I imagine they can be purchased from glossy show rooms or from the marble exhibition halls—products of the system, all the same one after the other, extruded all from a like mould. The *Integrity* was not one of them and she should never have fallen into the hands of people whose minds were set in those terms. She was a distinguished lady of immaculate breeding and she deserved to be treated as such. The art of building boats has changed over the years, adapting itself— successfully it must be said—to our new ways of life. I am the last to decry new ideas and new designs. I have known and

43

been on board fine modern vessels that anyone would be proud to sail in—strong, seaworthy, fast, safe. I have no sentimental reverence for the old—some old vessels are fine examples, embodying the best traditions. Others are preserved and honoured more for the sake of their antiquity than their real worth. But there are two distinct attitudes of mind that must be applied on the one hand to the contemporary and on the other to the traditional, two distinctive approaches to two different creatures—the two must be differently understood. When the lines get crossed no good will come of it. The *Integrity* was sold to a syndicate of three. They formed a company called Integrity Charters Incorporated and after each of the partners had sailed the schooner for one weekend, they sent her off on a voyage to Grenada with a delivery crew aboard.

It is no part of my business to apportion blame for what happened on that voyage—blame, for the most part, is irrelevant. What is important is the end result and whether any person may or may not have acted wrongly cannot affect the issue. Mostly we do what we think right. Some may have a greater awareness than others of the implications of a situation—more knowledge, more experience, a keener judgment. Some may be more level headed than others, more able to act coolly, more resistant to the sea's remorseless and constant pressures. At sea and ashore, most of the decisions we make are not acts of incisive thinking embracing in a single sweep every facet of a situation and foreseeing every sequel. Rather they are the piece-meal build up of a hundred small judgments, each in themselves of little consequence but together leading us on step by step, motivated perhaps by a deeper, almost a pyschological desire that guides us with frightening certainty. Then, when the final cry comes, "Abandon Ship!" it has been made inevitable by what has gone before. So it was with the *Integrity*.

There were six in the delivery crew—a professional seaman who had been employed as Master to deliver the yacht to Grenada, an English couple, Frank and Beryl West who were to

44

be the *Integrity's* skipper and cook for chartering in the Grenadines, two from South Dartmouth, Mark and Peter—the only two who had ever been on board before—and another young American. The crew had never sailed together before, they knew very little about the boat and her gear and they none of them had experience of deep water sailing in a vessel of the *Integrity's* type. If she had been a modern ketch or sloop with all the familiar gear—sheet winches, levers for the runners, roller reefing, light terylene or dacron sails, a protected cockpit with a dog-house and dodgers, stanchions and guard rails—it might have been a happier story. For a scratch crew to handle a heavy wooden ship designed and built with no concessions to modern handiness, on a long ocean passage in winter, was asking too much. Just as the *Integrity* had been unashamedly conceived as a throw-back to another era, so to handle her, to understand her and to master her complexities would call for seamanship of a kind that is rare in these days. With a crew thrown together more by chance and by random choice than by any clear understanding of the task before them it would have been remarkable if she had arrived safely in Grenada.

She sailed in October 1970, coasted south the four hundred odd miles to Chesapeake Bay and then took the Intercoastal waterway to skirt round inside Cape Hatteras and Cape Lookout as far as Moorhead City. She made her departure from the Beaufort Inlet on November 2nd, bound for St. Thomas in the American Virgin Islands, 1,250 miles to the south east as the crow flies. She was not alone. *Migette, Wanderlust, Kittiwake* and the motor yacht *Jim Hawkins,* were all bound for St. Thomas and all left Moorhead City at about the same time as the *Integrity.* The North Atlantic ocean in November is not a hospitable place as the crews were soon to discover.

A coincidence, second in its improbability only to my astonishing encounter with Waldo in Scotland, was my meeting with Frank West. I had started work on this story and had ferreted out a fair amount of information about the *Integrity*—the more I found the more tantalising the gaps became. I

45

lacked an authentic account of the schooner's abandonment, by someone who had been on board. Apart from three articles in the American magazine *Yachting* there was little to go on. The articles were written in part by one of the directors of Integrity Charters Inc. and in part by a journalist. Neither had been on board *Integrity* when the events took place. In common with the world at large, my understanding of what happened was confined to this source. A magazine article is a bad basis on which to form judgments. By its nature, magazine reporting is a subjective art and in addition, the wild and harrowing adventures which the crew of the *Integrity* lived through must have made it difficult for them to give an accurate and rational description. All that I knew with certainty was what happened to them and what happened to the *Integrity*. Like everyone else whose interests had been aroused by the schooner—those who knew her well, those who had seen her, those who only knew of her—I had no option but to accept the story as told in the magazine.

One winter day when I was sitting at home in my attic room, gazing across the Essex countryside and striving to piece together the details of the *Integrity's* story from any source I could find, the telephone rang. It was a friend asking me to his house. Other friends were there, one a writer. We discussed the politics and pitfalls of the trade. "What are you working on now?" he said. "A book about an American schooner—the *Integrity*." "That's odd", he said, "there is a friend of mine in the yacht marina who was aboard her when she was wrecked." For a moment I was silenced by astonishment. "What?" I stammered. I had followed every clue I had been able to gather—I had written countless letters, I had scoured yacht club lists, I had made a journey abroad on a false trail. Here on my doorstep was what I wanted—the marina was half a mile from where we stood. My friend and I left the party at once. We found Frank West on the new boat he had built himself—preparing her for a voyage from Essex to Nova Scotia. Frank told me what I believe to be the truth about the events of that November day. In some respects his

46

story differs from the account in the magazine article.

In the afternoon of November 2nd the *Integrity* cleared the buoy off Beaumont Inlet and set course to cross the Gulf Stream more or less at right angles. The forecast was for south-westerly winds up to Force 6. It was a reasonable forecast and gave no cause for excessive caution although the general weather pattern was unsettled. It was typical Gulf Stream weather for November. For the first two days she made good progress, sailing fast through a rough sea with the wind on the starboard beam. Once across the Gulf Stream she would make her easting way out into the Atlantic and then she would turn south to pick up the trade wind on her port bow. On the third day the weather began to deteriorate. The forecasters gave warning of a north-westerly gale with winds up to Force 8. In fact the wind backed to NNW and increased to Force 9 or 10. The *Integrity* was in trouble. Her position was Lat. 29° 44½′ N and Long. 72° 02′ W.

On the face of it, Frank West told me, there was nothing to worry about. The seas at that time did not seem dangerous—the schooner was running fast, perhaps too fast, under a staysail sheeted well in. There were two on watch, Frank himself and Mark, one of the boys from South Dartmouth; the rest of the crew were below in the main cabin, some asleep in their bunks and some sitting round the big scrubbed table. It was heavily overcast with wisps of low, grey cloud racing across the sky below the main cover. By this time she had made 395 miles, an average of 6 knots—about what one would expect of a vessel like the *Integrity*.

Frank told me that the schooner was laid over by a sea some time before she met the two waves that knocked her down and damaged her. She was running with the wind on the starboard quarter when she missed her footing, gave a sudden lurch to port and buried the lee deck. There was no damage, she recovered herself quickly, but one of the ports in the cabin top, giving on to the accommodation for'ard, had been left open and the sea poured in flooding Peter's bunk and forcing him to move to the fo'c'sle—a move that must have saved him from serious injury. Perhaps it was a warning that the schooner was being driven too hard. She might have been easier with less sail, running under bare poles or hove-to. All these events took place well inside the Bermuda Triangle where many strange things are said to have happened and where freak weather conditions have often been encountered.

The *Integrity* was becoming difficult to steer—she began to need a lot of helm to keep her on course. Frank and Mark stood one each side of the wheel, passing the spokes from one to the other, watching her bow and checking her as she tried to sheer into the wind. Neither of them were wearing life jackets or safety harnesses. It was a mad, exhilarating rush down wind. The schooner was hurtling across the seas like a racer with the bit in her teeth, slightly out of control. Every man who follows the sea must sooner or later go through the experience of a severe gale. From it is bred the mature seaman—the man who can anticipate danger and allow for it, who can accurately weigh the risks for his crew and his boat against the power of the sea and bring them safely through.

Experiences at sea lend themselves to exaggeration. Strong winds become gales in the telling, gales hurricanes, moderate seas become huge, big waves giants. Although I do not believe it has ever been documented or scientifically analysed, there is no doubt of the existence of rogue waves. Anyone sailing the oceans, whether in big ships or small, will notice that occasionally a wave or a pair of waves is, for no discernible reason, bigger and more powerful by far than those preceding or following it. I have never heard a satisfactory explanation of this fact—all I know is that it is fact because I have experienced it.

Frank West told me that in some way he felt the presence of the wave that wrecked the *Integrity* before he saw it. He turned round involuntarily and looked astern in time to see a wall of water, slightly concave, rearing up behind the yacht, high above him. It seemed to be advancing on the *Integrity* with individual intent—it wasn't very long, he said, but high so that he was looking directly up at it. The top of the wave

48

was all unsteady, beginning to break and totter. Suddenly the whole crazy mass of crest broke apart and seemed to explode, dragged away from the main body of wave by the tearing wind. He felt the stern of the yacht lift as if a great hand had clutched her from under the sea and thrust her upwards. He yelled to Mark, "Look out Mark—hold on man"— then tons of water descended on them from above.

It was too late for any action, the wave was on them— Frank could only yell and grab for the most immediate solid object, the wheel. He threw both his arms round the spokes and held on with all his strength. He felt the dead weight of water fall on top of him and then he was submerged under a rushing torrent which pressed him against the wheel. He could see the spokes and the binnacle and the outline of the hatch and the deckhouse in front of him all under the sea, distorted and hazy and out of perspective. He seemed to hold on for a long time and then the tearing pressure of water wrenched him loose from his hold and suddenly he was himself hurtling free over the side, turned this way and that under the sea, ropes and spars and the outline of the schooner's deck cartwheeling before his eyes.

The first wave knocked the schooner on her side and laid her over so that her masts were in the water. The dinghy was wrenched out of its davits which were themselves torn from their fastenings and was smashed against the taffrail with such force that a whole section of it was carried away. The force of the falling water had smashed the main boom which, with the mainsail furled and lashed to it, had been held up by its topping lift. The foresail gaff had been broken in the same way.

Frank West came to the surface, gasping for breath, in time to see the second wave strike the *Integrity*. This time she was overwhelmed completely. He found himself in the sea abaft the main mast about ten feet away from the schooner's deck which was almost in the vertical plane. Loose gear and loose rope was floating all about him. The masts were still clear of the water. The second wave hit the exposed bilge and swept under the stern, at the same time lifting the schooner and

49

pressing her further over. Frank saw the masts hit the surface of the sea. He watched with a kind of detached fascination as she began to roll over, as if he was not himself concerned with her. He remembers clearly that he saw the neat wooden box which housed the steering compass, which had been positioned on the deckhouse for'ard of the wheel, floating away almost within his grasp. He felt that he ought to get this box back—grabbed for it and tried to swim after it. But the wind took it far out of his reach and his legs became tangled with a rope lying across the surface of the water. And then he turned and saw that the schooner had rolled her masts under—perhaps 10° beyond the horizontal or perhaps more—until he could see the edge of her keel across the hull.

She seemed to hesitate, undecided whether to roll right over or whether to swing back. For a few moments he watched her as she made up her mind and then, at first very slowly, she began to come back. As she began to lift herself clear of the sea Frank swam a few strokes towards the main mast, seized the after shroud and held on. The schooner lifted herself, gathering momentum as she came. He was lifted with her and when she jerked upright he was shaken from the rigging and landed in a heap on the after deck. The force of the sea broke the main top-mast at the hounds and it came crashing down like a huge lance, thudding into the deck within feet of where Frank lay. He gathered himself and ran to the wheel looking round for Mark.

In some way Mark had been caught up in the loose main sheet as the first wave struck and when the boom snapped he had been lifted off the deck by it and was held suspended with the rope round his body, pressed to the spar and the sail. He too had been carried under water, trapped like an insect in a web. He too had waited as the *Integrity* hesitated, wondering which way she would choose to go. As she righted herself the sheet had suddenly fallen slack and Mark had dropped back to the deck. It was as if the schooner had taken pains to keep him safe. He ran to the wheel and with Frank, they spun the spokes to port. The fore staysail filled and the

50

schooner gathered her way once more leaving a litter of broken hatches and smashed gear floating in the sea behind her.

Wind force, in common with the size of waves and a yacht's angle of heel is a topic highly susceptible of exaggeration—what any yachtsman says on any of these subjects should normally be divided by two. On this occasion there is little doubt that the wind was blowing at least a full gale and that the seas were steep and dangerous. Freak seas are by no means so rare in the Bermuda Triangle as in many parts of the ocean. In calm weather, in depths of two thousand fathoms I have seen the sea strangely agitated as if in a tide rip or shallow water and Frank West told me he had seen the same. In a gale this sort of phenomenon spells dangerous, destructive waves.

While the *Integrity* was living through these fateful hours the other yachts in her close vicinity, although not in touch with her, were also suffering extreme conditions. The ketch *Wanderlust* was knocked down by a wave. The owner, his wife and eighteen-year-old son were on board. The owner had been steering for a long time and was tired. The yacht was running at seven knots under bare poles. When the weather began to improve the owner lashed the wheel and went below for a cup of coffee. Almost at once the yacht was overwhelmed by a sea and was knocked on her side. She recovered immediately but the three of them were thrown across the cabin. They were not badly hurt. The *Kittiwake* arrived in St. Thomas very late, was overdue and presumed lost by the U.S. Coastguard who informed the crew's families. One of them telephoned his home on arrival to be greeted as one returned from the dead. The motor cruiser *Jim Hawkins* left slightly ahead of the others and missed the worst of the gale. *Migette* had a rough time but came through without undue anxiety.

The frequency of winds Force 8-9 in that part of the North Atlantic in October to November is only 2%-3%, the sea that overwhelmed the *Integrity* is described in the magazine as a freak wave and at one point as a "mammoth, maverick wave".

The angle of heel is variously given as 10° past the horizontal and, incredibly, 180°. Waldo believes that properly handled, his schooner could have survived any gale provided she had sea room. Running before the wind under drastically reduced sail, streaming warps if necessary, she ought to have been as comfortable as a railway train. Alternatively, she might have been better hove-to, so that her rather weak stern and that pulling boat perched up above it were out of danger. She would heave-to easily under a backed fore staysail.

Apart from Frank and Mark on watch, the crew were in the main cabin for'ard when the wave struck, relaxed and unprepared for disaster. The motion was slow and steady, almost restful in its regular rhythm. As she ran down wind the schooner would swing gently and easily to port, stay for a moment at the limit of her roll poised on her natural point of balance and then swing back through the perpendicular and down to starboard in like manner. The crew were well used to it—there was a timeless metre to it which was soothing. Through the open hatch the diminished roar of the sea was a soft and sleepy harmony. Peter, whose bunk had been soaked an hour earlier, had fallen peacefully to sleep in one of the cots in the forepeak, his thoughts far away in Dartmouth, Massachusetts. The *Integrity* was at her best when running free when her heavy displacement made her a steady, comfortable ship. Then, in seconds, all was chaos and wild confusion. She rolled to port more suddenly perhaps and with a hint of violence which they had not felt before. As she paused to change her gait, in the way she always paused, the wave hit her and she rolled on. The settled and orderly world of a ship's cabin at sea sprung apart. The crew first looked at one another in astonished disbelief then flung out their arms in a vain attempt to grasp at any solid thing. They tumbled to the lee side as the cabin tilted to an altogether unprecedented angle in a crazy avalanche of people and things. The drink cabinet sprung from the bulkhead, flung open its doors and rained bottles and glasses and decanters. Pots and pans, plates, cutlery, lamps, chairs, books, the radio took to

52

the air and flew across the main cabin. The cabin sole opened upwards and two of the massive paving blocks which Waldo had put in for ballast, tumbled out and crashed to the lee side, smashing everything in their path. The noise was deafening. The main battery box came loose and lunged across the engine room, from above could be heard the roar of rushing water and the crash of breaking spars and rigging. The light from the hatches was darkened by sea, the main skylight was wrenched from its fastenings and swept overboard. From their random positions the crew looked up not at the deck-head but at the cabin sole arching over them. By a miracle no one was badly hurt. Peter was thrown out of his bunk in the forepeak, found himself under a deluge of water and struggled through it, swimming and hauling with his hands towards the companionway. When the schooner righted herself the crew picked themselves up, grabbed for life jackets and scrambled to the deck.

They were a badly shaken crew, not without reason. They were mostly young and comparatively inexperienced. Their ship had been damaged, irreparably it may have seemed to them. There was water below, the main topmast had come crashing to the deck, the main boom was broken as was the foresail gaff and the pulling boat had been wrenched out of its davits and smashed. Some ballast had shifted. The stone paving blocks had broken through the cabin sole and had crashed across the ship. One had fetched up against the bunk Peter had been sleeping in before he moved to the fo'c'sle smashing the stout wooden bunkboard to matchwood and destroying the bunk itself. Nothing appears more alarming than damage to a sailing vessel, nothing strikes panic into the heart more surely than the disarray of broken gear and a loose tangle of rope spread over the deck. It is frightening when the order and logic of a boat is torn to pieces, suddenly and irrevocably and replaced by chaos. The very order of things—one's life, one's only link with the world of home and people and ordinary living is suddenly put at risk. A boat in her proper element and properly at ease in it, even though

53

conditions may be appalling, is reassuring and gives off security and comfort. A man can revel in her grace of movement, her skill as she dances through the storm, threading her way surefooted and nimble over and among the tumbling mountains of destructive ocean. If anything goes wrong the whole basis of life is cast into doubt, the ocean takes on a sinister aspect. When Beryl stood up on the poop deck and shouted, "A ship—a ship—I can see a ship", because they were young or inexperienced or lacked heart, they failed to understand that to come through against the sea's wrath you must hang on and hang on until you reach the bitter end. The apprehensions of the *Integrity's* crew took charge of their reason and they fired off red distress rockets. It was the schooner's undoing.

The main topmast had come crashing to the deck, the main boom was broken as was the fores'l gaff, and the pulling boat had been wrenched from its davits and smashed.

CHAPTER VI

Once the rockets had been fired the *Integrity's* skipper had lost the power of choice, he was no longer master of the situation, he would now be rescued whether he liked it or not regardless of what happened to his own ship in the process, regardless of his own wishes. An operation had been set in motion that he could not easily arrest or control and which spelled disaster for the *Integrity*. It may be that he himself did not give explicit instructions for the rockets to be fired— some other member of the crew, hearing Beryl's cry and being infected by the heady fever of panic, may have taken this irreversible initiative. Frank West said he thought the skipper's intention was for the ship to do no more than stand by until the extent of the damage could be established. It happened that she arrived at the precise moment when the situation on board the *Integrity* was full of confusion—when her crew was recovering, as best they could, from what must have been a major shock. The yacht was in chaos—the crew were frightened and had not had time to pull themselves together. They were taken aback, bemused. It seemed incredible that so fine and strong a vessel could have been brought to such a state by a single stroke. The *Integrity* had seemed so massive, so enormously invulnerable. Now the big hatch over the main cabin had gone leaving a gaping hole, open to the sea. The decks were a jumble of broken spars and torn gear. In fact the *Integrity* was in no way seriously damaged. She had suffered a knock-down, broken a couple of spars and the main topmast, lost the pulling boat, smashed some of the hatches and there was a little water in her but she was afloat, sound in all her timbers and tight—a fact which she was to demonstrate convincingly over the next few months. The main damage to her was in the engine room. The big wooden box on the starboard side which contained the starter batteries had been wrenched from its fastenings, thrown across the alleyway and wedged, upside down behind the engine, making it impossible for the engine to be started. The situation was serious but in no way desperate. There was no hostile land under the *Integrity's* lee—she could have been snugged down under bare poles and left to run down wind until the weather moderated, even if her steering gear had been damaged. Then, with five strong men on board, the batteries could have been put back in their place and the engine made serviceable. There was nothing wrong with it— all it lacked was power to get it going and she had fuel enough on board to take her into harbour. Alternatively, if the engine could not be made to work, she could have been sailed to the nearest port. Where she had come from, Morehead City and Nassau, Bahamas, were equidistant—she could have gone to Nassau under a jury rig which would have offered the likelihood of a fair wind. Even without a fair wind she could have made port. There was no hurry, she had stores and water on board, there was no injury to the crew. If the main boom had been broken beyond repair it could have been unshipped and the sail used loose footed. If the foresail could not be used the *Integrity* carried a fisherman staysail which in any reasonably moderate wind would have given her plenty of power. Her lockers were full of spare sails, rope and gear of every description. She was a very well found ship.

A well found yacht at sea is not easy to sink unless she is run foul of some solid object—the shore, another ship, a large piece of drifting wood, a whale, a buoy. Yachts have been lost through all these causes but very few through stress of the sea alone. Even in hurricanes, time and again the boats that are destroyed are the ones left in harbour or against the shore—those with sea room to ride it out survive. Throughout time sailing vessels struck by sudden and unpredictable weather, or vessels that are being driven too hard, have suffered their sails blown out, or dismasting or damage to gear or some accident such as stove-in hatches or shifting cargo, but very few have sunk from the weather alone. Yachts have been knocked down, like the *Integrity* was, they have turned turtle, they have been pitchpoled as the Smeetons were in the Southern Ocean but they have usually managed to crawl into port to make repairs. A sailing vessel, unlike a steamer or a power boat which is able to push itself against the wind and the weather by artificial, mechanical means, always gives to the sea, is always taken with the weather so that her resistance to it is always diminished. The sea is tolerant of those who understand its power and who do not attempt, through foolishness or arrogance, to match it. The key to survival in a storm is sea room—given plenty of space with nothing in the way the only enemy a seaman has is his own nerve. His ship, even his life, will depend on his ability to act coolly and resourcefully, to see that his crew act in a like manner and not to be influenced by them if they try to rush him into false decisions.

Nothing is easier than to relax in the comfort of an armchair and judge another man for decisions taken on the windswept, heaving deck of a damaged yacht in a gale. The skipper's first responsibility is to his crew. It may be that to save his ship he has to risk his crew and if the risk is not forced on him, he may not think it justifiable. If the *Bela Krajina* had not appeared there would have been no decision to make—the crew would have borne it out and they would have come through with their ship. But having seen the *Bela Krajina*—being presented out of nothing with the sudden offer of assistance, who is to say that the skipper should not have taken it? If he had turned it down and then found that the *Integrity* was sinking and beyond his capacity to repair, where would he find another ship to take his crew to safety in this limitless expanse of ocean? If he had refused assistance and had then lost his crew, or even one member of his crew, he would have been most harshly blamed.

There are several options open to the skipper who finds himself at sea in a storm. He can heave-to, he can lie a-try, he can run under bare poles, he can lie to a sea anchor over the bow or over the stern, he can stream warps, he can use an oil bag to quell the seas, he can strip the windage off his ship by taking down loose halyards and gear from aloft, he can lie a-hull with no sail up, allowing the boat to look after herself. Having done any one or several of these things, except run before it, he should be able to go below with an easy mind, brew himself hot, strong tea and go to sleep until the holocaust is over and better times break through. If the wind is favourable he will decide to run before it because in that way he is making valuable miles towards his destination which is good for morale. If he elects to keep going in this way he will get no rest—a boat running down wind before a gale must be watched. But to run down wind is probably the safest choice. End-on to the seas and going with them a boat is safe provided she is going more slowly than the breaking crests—if she is going too fast she will surf, perhaps for as long as half a minute on one wave and then she will be out of control, she will not answer her helm and she will be in danger of broaching. I remember that I looked round at the frenzied sea when *Iskra* was running through a gale in the Atlantic and understood completely that if this happened she would stand no chance whatsoever of surviving.

Most yachts are surprisingly quiet and still down below while the gale rages outside. Hiscock states, quite un-dogmatically, that he believes a yacht of about thirty tons, the size of the *Integrity*, is safer than any other in a storm. A smaller, modern vessel, he thinks, may be overwhelmed by the sheer size and power of the seas. My own view is that an

58

Iskra sized yacht (ten tons) is as safe if she is heavy and full in her for'ard section. Modern yachts, which after all are not generally designed to grapple with storm conditions, often have a fine entry and having less buoyancy for'ard, might tend to bury their noses and be pitchpoled in a heavy following sea. If the seas the *Integrity* met on November 5th were comparable with those that assailed *Iskra* in the same piece of ocean a few months later, the distance between crests was not more than 80 yards and the height of the waves not more than 35 feet. In the Southern Ocean, where the fetch of the seas is infinite, these dimensions can be 100 yards and 50 feet respectively. I was once off Cape Horn in a steamer and the sight of the storm was something that can never be forgotten. The experience served to place the size and length of seas in perspective for me and I now judge all other waves by the memory of those waves. Hundreds of yachts have sailed round Cape Horn, many of them in conditions unthinkable in softer latitudes but as far as I know none have foundered through stress of the weather.

The skipper had gathered his crew together on deck and put them to work after the knock down. Two had been set to the hand pumps on the deck, sitting one each side on the break of the poop and working purposefully at the big capacity Edson bilge pumps. The water gushed out, ran over the deck and through the scuppers as the *Integrity* rolled—hard work but productive. In half an hour the ship was dry. Covers were devised for the broken hatches with wood and canvas ripped from the bunk covers, although there was plenty of spare canvas in the store. The skipper cut away the stove-in boat which was streaming from the davits by one fall, smashing itself against the ship's side every time the *Integrity's* stern rose to a sea. He cleared away the falls, throwing the lines clear of the steering gear. Then he climbed aloft up the wooden ratlines to bring some order into the tangle of gear that hung round the mast like Christmas decorations. The broken topmast was standing with its heel on the deck held by a shroud and its jumper stay and swinging crazily from side to side as the yacht rolled. He squared up as best he could and lashed the broken spar to the shrouds. While he was aloft, inexplicably, the steering lines parted and the wheel spun slack and useless. Perhaps the gear had been damaged when the boat was stove-in or perhaps the wheel had been fouled by the broken main boom. The skipper improvised a quick repair. Ropes were led through the blocks in the bulwarks from the tiller head so that two men could steer, one heaving and one slacking to keep the yacht on course. The advantage of Captain Culler's and Slocum's steering gear is its basic simplicity. But now it was back-breaking work with the wind and the seas still rising. Two men could stand no more than ten minutes of it. It was ten minutes in every half hour and it seemed to go on for ever. The respite between tricks was not long enough, it was wet and it was cold. The concentration, the bending and heaving at the lines, the violent motion, the feeling that it was a fight against all the odds wore the crew out, exhausting them, demoralising them and destroying their will.

Only Beryl saw the ship—ahead of the *Integrity* to the south. The others looked in partial disbelief in response to her cry, straining their eyes through the mist and rain squalls towards a murky, indistinct horizon. Frank West thinks that if the ship had shown herself half an hour later or earlier the rockets would never have been fired. Fright and fatigue are compulsive and pervasive masters.

The ship hove in sight at mid-day. She was the *Bela Krajina*, a Yugoslav freighter bound for Sundalova, Norway, with a full cargo of coal from the Gulf, in command of Captain Vlajki. She lumbered towards them towering above through the mist and blown spray, rolling drunkenly in the heavy seas, grey and overpowering and offering at the same time safety and destruction, a haven, warmth and the smell of coffee and dry blankets, and also the ultimate danger. She came deliberately, an unwieldy colossus, blocking out the light as she passed slowly along the *Integrity's* side. The crew looked up and saw rows of faces peering down at them like visitors from

60

She lumbered towards them through the mist and blown spray.

another planet—shouting unintelligibly in a foreign tongue, gesticulating, advising, remonstrating. A line was thrown—they saw it snake out against the sky, hang for an instant poised above them, catch against a flying stay and then fall clear and drop into the sea. The freighter passed ahead and the *Integrity's* crew watched fascinated as she turned in a great circle to windward and came in for a second time. Again a line was hurled, again it fell impotent into the sea, again the freighter circled and again—each time the line failed as if the *Integrity,* conscious of her danger, affronted and defiant was nimbly dodging away from an insufferable indignity.

It is hard to imagine what use would have been made of the line if it had ever been secured aboard the *Integrity.* A tow? In those seas and at that distance from port, impossible.

61

Yachts can never be towed by ships except for short distances, at slow speeds, in calm weather and ideal conditions. The towing vessel, unmanoeuvrable and disposing of too much power, inevitably tows too fast. The yacht invariably finds herself in difficulties—her deck fittings carried away where the tow line is made fast, or shipping water as she is dragged through the seas, or her trim altered by the weight of the towing gear or unable to steer and sheering off to one side or the other. To take the crew off? The chances of heaving a man from the deck of a yacht to a ship on a rope are slender. It can be done if conditions are good but it is difficult and dangerous. It is not clear what were the intentions of the *Integrity's* skipper. He could not use the yacht's radio telephone—it had come adrift and had smashed in the knock-down. With it he could have spoken with the *Bela Krajina*—there must have been someone on board who spoke English even if, as seems unlikely, the ship's radio officer did not. On the telephone the skipper could have put whatever plan he had to the ship's captain and it could have been worked out in co-operation. Instead, the skipper shouted up at the *Bela Krajina's* bridge towering above him, his voice half drowned by the roar of the wind. With both vessels travelling through the water at some speed it is hard to see what he could have done with the *Bela Krajina's* rope except to have used it to transfer one or two members of his crew on a life raft. It might have been possible. A raft could have been ready on deck, the *Integrity* had at least one on board, and as the ship came past and threw her a line it could have been made fast and the raft allowed to swing alongside the ship. If he had been able to transfer any crew member who wanted to leave, the skipper would have saved his ship.

After three attempts to pass a line the *Bela Krajina* pulled clear and waited—possibly for some sign from the yacht, some indication of her intention. Then, for the first time, the *Integrity* was hove-to. Her tiller was lashed to leeward, the fore staysail was hove a-weather and she swung into the trough of the seas and lay quiet. This must be the signal. Now

Captain Vlajki knew what was expected of him, understood what he was being asked to do. He placed his ship athwart the wind on the *Integrity's* weather side, rolling heavily and drifting sideways down towards the yacht. The crew hung ladders over the side, stood by with ropes and life jackets and waited. Too late the *Integrity's* skipper saw his danger—understood suddenly the extent of the disaster that was about to overtake him. The towering iron side of the *Bela Krajina* advanced on the *Integrity* yard by inevitable yard, the whole edifice heaving itself towards her and then rolling dizzily away before the next mad lurch brought her closer and yet closer. The crew of the *Integrity* looked up in terror at the towering iron wall, pitted and slimy with rust and weed, the lines of rivets disappearing upwards and sideways into infinity. Plunged into calm by the ship's bulk, relieved suddenly of the steadying wind the *Integrity* rolled as she had never rolled before, dipping her rails under and flooding the deck with water, the masts sweeping from side to side in a great arc, ever closer to the advancing ship. Now, her wind taken away from her and with no engine, she was helpless. The crew yelled in alarm. The ladders swung giddily out over the *Integrity* and then were hurled back against the ship's side with a sickening clatter. No man dared to grapple with them.

Then the *Integrity's* gear begun to run foul of the freighter's deck. First the jumper stay between the masts caught on some deck projection as the yacht rolled and broke, carrying away the unused aerial at the foremast head. Captain Vlajki seeing that the crew would not or could not jump to safety, rang slow ahead in an effort to move his ship clear. The *Integrity's* crew heard the engine room telegraph, felt the vibration of the ship's engines. As she gathered her way the *Integrity* moved down the iron side with increasing speed. First the foremast caught under the freighter's rail. There was an awful rending. The mast broke off at the deck— the forestay snapped—the broken heel of the mast slid up the deck gouging a channel in the planking—broken wires and ropes flew dangerously about—the foremast came to rest leaning drunkenly against the main mast—the crew ran aft or crouched in the scuppers to avoid the hail of broken gear from aloft—the ship's crew yelled down from above. The *Integrity* rolled sickeningly away from the ship and then, gathering strength she rolled back. Now she was fighting an unconquerable foe—she had tried to escape, now that she was trapped she turned and fought back with all the courage her creators had passed over to her. She lunged again, now with her mainmast. The truck, below the stump of the already broken topmast fouled under an iron davit. There was another terrible rending of wood and rope and wire and now the yacht's gear—the glory of sail and spar and wire and rope that makes of a sailing vessel one of man's supreme creations— came crashing down on deck and into the sea alongside. Only the crew's shouts could be heard above the rage of destruction. Dismasted and in turmoil the *Integrity* made a last lunge at her tormentor. As she came past the *Bela Krajina's* stern, in way of the threshing propellers, she struck with her last weapon. The bowsprit and the flying jib-boom—Captain Culler's pride—became meshed under the freighter's counter. A last Atlantic wave, impersonal and impartial in the majesty of its immense power, bore down the freighter's stern until the schooner's fine bow was broken with a shattering, splintering report that seemed to the yacht's crew to echo round the ocean's bleak mansion. Now the *Integrity* was finished, reduced to a hulk, her finery lying across the deck and in the sea around her. Now for the first time her skipper had no choice—all his options had been used or set aside— there was only one road open to him. For him and his crew to survive they would have to be taken off the *Integrity*.

CHAPTER VII

The *Integrity* was of no concern to Captain Vlajki of the Yugoslav ship *Bela Krajina*—he had no interest in her, no feelings for her except, possibly, of irritation, annoyance and frustration. He was irritated because she seemed incapable of helping herself, annoyed because she was delaying his passage, causing expense and extra work for his crew for no good reason that he could see and causing him to attempt the near impossible—to manoeuvre his ship, heavy and sluggish with a full cargo of coal, in a gale alongside a tiny wooden vessel as frail as an egg shell in comparison. He was frustrated because everything he did seemed to evoke no seamanlike response from the *Integrity*. He knew that when he did, eventually, take the *Integrity's* crew aboard they would be nothing but an inconvenience to him. He would be forced to make an additional call on his way across the Atlantic in order to put them off again with all the attendant expense and delay. For his pains he would get no thanks from the Splosna Plovba, the state shipping line that his ship belonged to. There was no possibility, it seemed, that he could come out of the affair with any advantage. But red distress rockets had been seen—all his instincts as a seaman, hammered in, age after age, by the remorseless indoctrination of the sea itself, demanded of him that if life was at stake at sea he must use his every endeavour to save it. It is an inviolable rule of the ocean, from which wise men and fools profit equally and which cuts across nationality, colour, class and all considerations of worth and virtue, that human life is paramount and that no expense or inconvenience must be spared when it comes to snatching souls from Davy Jones's locker.

The Captain had been in his day cabin when the bridge telephone rang. The second mate, Mr. Lončaric, had picked up an echo on the radar—a small vessel of some kind, possibly a fishing boat. He had not himself seen any signal but the stand-by man, climbing the bridge ladder from the galley had seen the *Integrity* through a brief break in the low cloud scudding across the turbulent, grey surface of the sea. He had seen, he said, two red distress rockets. By the time the Captain had climbed the stairway to the wheelhouse the radar screen was clear and there was no sign of any vessel from either wing of the bridge. It was already blowing Force 8 and visibility was poor—the *Bela Krajina* had the seas on her port quarter and she was beginning to roll heavily. Although she was heavy and low in the water, every time she pitched her propeller would race and the whole ship would shake with the vibration. The ship was making good speed but the Captain knew that she would soon have to be slowed down. The Chief had already been on the engine room telephone. The Captain questioned the stand-by man closely. Was he certain he had seen red rockets? "Yes sir." What sort of boat was it? "It had two masts—some sort of a yacht sir." The Captain sent for the radio officer. Had he been listening during the past half hour? "Yes sir." Did anything come through on R/T? "No sir." The Captain thought hard. He had a mind to go on. Perhaps it was a false alarm—perhaps the yacht had been afraid of being run down and had let off rockets to draw attention to her position—perhaps the stand-by man had been mistaken. He had no stomach for turning his ship round and searching the ocean in these conditions. Then the stand-by man said, "There was a woman on the poop deck sir—she was waving her arms."

The *Bela Krajina* turned slowly into the wind. She rolled heavily to starboard as she came round and brought the wind against the full length and height of her slab side. A sea rolled over the deck for'ard of the bridge and tons of green water slopped to and fro until it drained through the freeing ports. The Second Mate and the Third came on the bridge, the watch below were called out to man the upper deck and scan the sea. The ship felt the full force of the gale when she turned into the wind—she pitched her bow into the face of a wave. With the deep-throated roar that a big sea makes when it breaks aboard a ship a piece of the Atlantic came rolling majestically over the fo'c'sle head cascading down into the for'ard well deck, submerging the whole fore part of the ship so that derricks, winches, rails, hatch coamings, ventilators, stood out stark and grim from the angry white foam. The ship gave an inner shudder as she felt the weight of it and then, slowly, the wave's pent-up energy was dissipated and spent in a drawn out rasping and hissing like the last breath of some giant ocean monster. The weather was still worsening. Captain Vlajki ordered the ship to be slowed down another ten revolutions.

It took nearly an hour before the *Integrity* was seen again on the radar screen—still no radio message came and still the yacht did not answer the *Bela Krajina's* call. Moments later visibility lifted and she could be seen ahead and to starboard. The Captain could see clearly through binoculars—the crew on deck, the two men steering with tiller lines, the woman waving from the poop. She was making a fair speed down wind—too fast it seemed to the Captain—under her fore staysail. She had obviously met with a serious accident—the crew were waving, clearly asking for assistance. The Captain slowed the ship's engines again until she barely had steerage way, moving slightly faster than the *Integrity*. Then, standing in the wing of the bridge and shouting his instructions to the man at the wheel he brought his ship close down the *Integrity's* side. The Bo'sun and his party under the Mate stood on the foredeck in front of the bridge and when the *Integrity* was fair alongside they fired a rocket line over her masts. The line caught in the rigging but no one secured it and as the ship moved past it fell clear. Three times the Captain turned his ship round through the wind's eye against the full force of those seas—three times the line was lost. Then the *Integrity* hove-to. The Captain lay off and waited and watched through the binoculars. As he watched it seemed to him that there could be only one reason for the yacht to heave-to—he was being asked to come alongside. Well, the yacht would be damaged—wrecked possibly—but that was no concern of his. He was being asked to take off the crew—there was no way in which he could save the yacht. He summoned the Mate to the bridge and they discussed it together. Ropes were got ready, extra ladders put over the side, the hands stood by. Handling his ship boldly, but with the gentle care that comes of experience, the Captain placed the *Bela Krajina* broadside to the seas close to windward of the *Integrity*. Then the engines were stopped. Slowly the ship drifted towards the yacht exactly in position. From the wing of the bridge the Captain watched as the *Integrity* lost her wind and his ship came down on her. He could see the crew on her deck, the woman on the poop, all in their life jackets, the broken steering gear, the hatches crudely repaired. She was a lovely yacht—some wealthy man's plaything. They should have more sense than to tempt the North Atlantic in winter.

The Captain knew perfectly well that yachts in America were for rich people to enjoy themselves. He felt a certain bitterness. He had been at sea all his life to earn a hard living—the world of the sea was a real world to him. He was answerable—if he cost the Splosna Plovba Company money, if he wasted the valuable time of a big ship in a senseless jaunt, he would be asked the reason why in no uncertain terms. It was all very well for people in yachts to play games with the ocean for pleasure, but when their games came to pieces through their own stupidity, professional sailors like him had to pick up the bits—and waste good money in the doing of it.

The Captain had wasted half a day already. He knew that he would have to get these people aboard if only to justify it. There were yachts in Yugoslavia as well—not so big and grand as this one, but yachts none the less—used for training young seamen. The Captain himself had been aboard one years ago as a cadet. But they were properly handled by skilled and experienced seamen who knew their job.

When the *Bela Krajina* drifted down to the *Integrity* so that the ladders were over her deck the yacht's crew held back. The woman was frightened—so much was clear. The Captain could see the *Integrity's* deck laid out in all its detail beneath him. They were all shouting but not one of them made a move to fasten a steadying line to the bottom of the ladder. It would have been easy—even the woman could have climbed aloft, the Mate's men on the foredeck had a dozen ropes over. Then the yacht drifted still closer and her gear began to foul the *Bela Krajina's* deckline. Now the chance was past. The Captain moved his ship ahead and the *Integrity's* masts came tumbling out of her. The Captain cursed. Now they were in a right mess. There were only two chances left—one was the big twenty-man life raft on the *Bela Krajina's* foredeck and the other was the ship's motor lifeboat.

He turned his ship yet again through the wind and lay close to the *Integrity* yet again, studying her from the bridge through the binoculars. Now, with her masts and gear lying on deck and in the sea around her the *Integrity* was rolling with frightening violence. Two or three of the crew had set themselves to work, cutting away at the tangle of rope and canvas which cluttered the deck so that it fell overboard on the weather side. The masts were secured against the yacht's side by heavy wire shrouds which the crew could not cut free. The broken bowsprit and jib-booms were hanging drunkenly over the bows held by the chain bobstay and the bowsprit shrouds. The fancy dolphin striker was gouging at the yacht's bow as she rolled and pitched. The weather showed no improvement—if anything the wind was stronger. The Captain watched the *Integrity's* crew as they worked on the giddily rolling deck with knives and an axe, striving to keep a foothold against the motion and the tearing, clawing wind. When they had cleared the deck he saw them go to a white life-raft which was lashed to the main deck-house and cut the lashings. Two of them hove the cannister over the lee side while a third made fast the painter and trip line. He saw the white cannister spring apart as the compressed air bottle released its charge, saw the raft slowly take shape and grow in size. As it grew the fierce wind seemed to attack it with particular malevolence—a gust got under it, suddenly it lifted and flew in the wind, twisting and turning like a child's windmill, tearing at the grommets which held the painter to the fabric until they broke and the raft went cartwheeling away across the waves towards an infinity of its own. Now, it seemed to the Captain, the *Integrity's* crew were at their wits' end. Someone was signalling with an electric torch but he could make no sense of it. The Mate on the foredeck was ready with the *Bela Krajina's* own raft—much bigger than the *Integrity's*—too big and unwieldy for the job it was now required to do. It was launched and paid out downwind towards the yacht while the ship was kept to windward, positioned so that the raft dropped alongside the *Integrity* where its painter was caught and made fast. But this raft, although bigger and heavier, was also torn against its rope by the force of the wind and turned upside down. The *Integrity's* crew were getting tired—they lacked the strength or the will to right it and bring it alongside. The Captain summoned the Third Mate, Mr. Tijen to the bridge.

Perhaps the Captain had known all along that in the end, when all else failed, he would have to launch one of his own lifeboats. It was the last thing he wanted to do. The gale was at its height. Further to the west a ship was breaking up in monstrous seas—the radio officer picked up her frantic signals. The *Bela Krajina* was rolling more heavily. The seas were breaking against the weather side as she lay hove-to, sometimes sweeping across the main deck with such force that no man could live there and then tumbling over the lee rail in an immense fall of green. From the boat deck the sea to leeward was all confusion as the ship broke the symmetry of the waves with her bulk, the sea leaping up the iron ship's side as if already clawing for prey. To launch a lifeboat would call for skill, courage and discipline of a high order. The Captain knew he was risking the lives of a whole boat's crew—as for the boat itself, he knew there was no chance of recovering it. The Third Mate received his instructions calmly and took his boat's crew to their stations. He was young, agile, strong and confident yet fully aware of his responsibility. He had also known since the *Integrity* was first sighted that in the end he would be needed. He had selected his men—he knew all their virtues and all their defects—and he had gone over in his mind every danger, every pitfall, every chance mishap that he might meet. He knew precisely what he was doing when he gave the order, "Lower away."

The Senhouse slips were knocked free from the canvas covered lines that held the lifeboat tight in the davits, the men on the quadrant handles began to turn together and then, as the boat swung free of the deck and as the ship rolled to port the falls were quickly lowered. Lifeboats were the Third Mate's own responsibility. He was a man who took his work seriously and everything was in good order—the hauling parts of the falls were neatly coiled in their boxes so that the heavy tackles ran free, the quadrants were properly greased, the gear in the boat had been checked and was in good order. Ship's boats are seldom used and often neglected. Their condition and efficiency are a barometer of the efficiency of the ship herself. As the *Bela Krajina* rolled the other way the lifeboat, suspended like a pendulum, swung violently in towards the iron side. At a signal the Third Mate stopped the lowering and the crew, fenders ready, cushioned the shock as the boat struck the ship. Then she rolled to port again and again she dropped. Now the pendulum was longer and the swing more violent—the men in the boat were shaken like pebbles in a tin. Again they cushioned the shock as the boat swung in but this time she swung unevenly and the bows hit the ship's side a crushing, splintering blow. The gunwale was split and broken but the damage was superficial. Now she was in the water for an instant and then snatched up again as the ship rolled and the waves receded. Now the for'ard fall was free, the heavy block swinging dangerously above, but the after block jammed solid in the ring and could not be moved. As the ship rolled again to starboard the boat was lifted by her stern, higher and higher, so that the bow, free of its fall, swung away from the ship and plunged into the sea. The crew slithered and tumbled towards the bow, striving for hand holds. The Third Mate at the tiller, found an axe with his right hand and jamming his feet against the heavy block to save himself from sliding for'ard, he struck blindly at the rope. The fall was bar tight, humming with strain, and then the axe bit deep—the rope stranded and with the next blow it parted and the boat fell free and crashed into the sea. By good fortune it fell the right way up. Bruised and bleeding the crew went to their tasks—carefully rehearsed beforehand. Oars were shipped for'ard and the boat slowly pulled to safety away from the ship's side. Two pumps cleared the bilge, the engine was cranked and started by one of the engineers in the crew.

As soon as the lifeboat was free of the *Bela Krajina's* lee she felt the force of the gale. A squall of rain was sweeping across the sea. The ship could be seen through the murk, towering, grey, indistinct and blurred in a pall of mist. It seemed to the Third Mate that she floated in some strange half world of her own, a phantom suspended in limbo between sea and sky. He felt suddenly alone. His crew were silent, their faces fraught with apprehension. The even beat of the lifeboat's engine gave him some comfort as he steered the boat before these huge, majestic crests. The *Integrity* could not at first be seen but the Third Mate had memorised her compass bearing before he left the ship. In minutes she hove in sight—quite near-to. The Third Mate brought the lifeboat close past her and then, looking over his shoulder and judging his chance, he opened the throttle and swung the boat hard round between crests. She rolled to port and then came up the next wave and mounted its summit, hurling spray away from her bows. The engine was slowed enough to keep steerage way and the lifeboat came almost to a stop no more than a few yards away from the *Integrity* and in as much lee as she could offer. On the *Bela Krajina's* bridge the Captain put the binoculars to one side and grunted his approval. "Good lad that," he said. He rang slow ahead on the engine room telegraph.

The crew of the *Integrity* were huddled round the stump of the mast. The deck was still covered in gear—sails, rope, broken spars, Captain Culler's neatly parcelled shrouds lying across the yacht in a tangle. The masts were over the weather side, lying alongside her like a deftly improvised sea anchor so that the yacht herself was quite in the trough, the force of the seas broken for her by the clutter to windward. The Third Mate shouted in English, "Jump—jump in the sea—swim." The crew of the *Integrity* hesitated.

It is a hard thing to abandon your ship and jump into the sea—there is a certain primitive fear attached to it—a finality, the knowledge that you can never return, that your life must take a new direction. I remember that when I jumped into the sea at Puerto Piqueran and left the *Girl Stella* to sink I felt as if a cold finger was feeling inside my body, seeking out my heart and marking it for life with the indelible signature of defeat. The sea, when it gets on top, can crush and grind a man until he is humbled and reduced by its persistent and inexorable power. If he is allowed to rise again he may come up the stronger and the wiser for the experience. Beryl jumped first, the others followed—the sea was strangely warm after the cold rain. They swam together in a bunch, their life jackets holding them high out of the water. To the Third Mate they looked like a group of strange sea mammals paddling their way across the ocean. Strong, friendly hands hauled them on board the lifeboat. They sat in a group amidships, silent and resigned. The fright had gone out of Beryl's eyes. The *Integrity's* skipper was suddenly at ease—

73

They swam together in a bunch, their life jackets holding them high out of the water.

the responsibility lifted from him. Now someone else would make the decisions—he would give himself up to the delicious luxury of doing what he was told. There could be no respite for the Third Mate. The job was only half done—the most difficult part still to come.

The *Bela Krajina* steamed quickly past the abandoned *Integrity*, past the lifeboat and took up a position to leeward. The Captain held his ship with her quarter to the seas. She would roll heavily in this position but it gave her a chance of keeping the main deck free of heavy water. The Third Mate watched again for his chance and then, when he saw a space between the marching regiments on either side of him he opened the throttle, put the tiller hard over and turned the lifeboat's stern to the wind. Soon he was abreast of the *Bela*

Krajina and in her lee. The Captain rang dead slow ahead and the lifeboat's bowman caught a light line thrown from the ship's main deck and made it fast. Now the lifeboat was being towed slowly through the water. A ladder came tumbling down from the main deck and the Third Mate eased the lifeboat in towards it. He leaned forward from the tiller and tapped Beryl on the shoulder. "You first," he said. Held by two of the boat's crew, one each side of her, Beryl stood up on the side thwart. The boat swung in on a swell, the ladder was suddenly there in front of her. "Now", the Third Mate shouted, "Up." Beryl grasped the ladder as high as she could reach, put her feet on the bottom rung and climbed up two steps. It was difficult. The ladder seemed all slack—when she tried to move her feet or her hands it seemed to go away from her—seemed to have no substance. Then the sea took the lifeboat far away from her so that she dangled in space, alone. In a moment the ladder was hurled against the ship's side. She held on for her life. The ladder swung clear—now the ship was rolling the other way. The ladder dipped deep in the waves—Beryl felt water rushing all round her, tearing at her, grasping her and pulling her with wet, cold force. Beryl held on. She came up again and gained another rung. At that moment the *Bela Krajina* shipped a heavy sea over the main deck. As it came thundering across, the men on deck jumped for safety—to the bridge ladder, the samson posts, up ventilators. The sea came solid across the deck and rolled to the lee rail where it fell in a heavy curtain down on Beryl and on the lifeboat. Beryl held on—her arms were crooked through the rungs of the ladder. Now she was petrified with fright—she couldn't move. All she could do was to hold—hold on with all the grit and stubborn doggedness that the Lord gives to women to help them through pain and suffering.

She was still there when the wave was gone in a smother of white. The men on deck came back to the rail and looked down anxiously. One of them jumped over the rail, shinned down the ladder, passed down beside Beryl until he was below her on the ladder, put his arm around her and levered her up.

She gained two rungs. He pushed her legs from below and she gained another rung. Then the lifeboat rose on a sea and was pushed in towards the ladder. Once again the ship rolled—the man on the ladder was caught between the boat and the ship's side—he was knocked sharply on the back of the head by the boat's gunwale—his grip released and he fell into the sea. As he sank the boat moved over him. He came up on the other side of the boat, still conscious. He shouted and the Third Mate in the stern sheets, heard him, grabbed him an instant before he was gone and pulled him aboard. Beryl gained another rung. Two of the men on deck reached down and grasped her by the hair. She cried out in pain as they pulled. She gained another rung. Then they could reach down under her arms and they lifted her up over the rail and on to the deck. One by one the people in the lifeboat gained the *Bela Krajina's* deck—first the crew of the *Integrity,* then the boat's crew and last of all the Third Mate, watching his chance, brought the boat under the ladder, left the tiller, jumped and shinned aloft with all his youthful agility.

The Captain turned the *Bela Krajina* on course for Bermuda, counting the cost and counting his blessings. He had wasted half a day, lost a valuable boat and a valuable life-raft. He would waste more time and incur more expense when he landed his survivors in Bermuda. He had saved the lives of those whose lives he had been asked to save and he had lost none of his own. Two of his crew had been injured, neither of them seriously. The Mate, Mr. Močnik, had been hit by a spar as the *Integrity* crashed against the *Bela Krajina's* side and one of the lifeboat's crew had fallen in the boat, injuring his back. Captain Vlajki summoned the Radio Officer and together they wrote out a signal to the U.S. Coastguard. He gave the news that he had taken off the crew of the American yacht *Integrity* in Lat. 29° 44½' N, Lon. 72° 02' W. He reported that he had left the yacht a derelict—a danger to shipping.

Third Officer Tijen is now Captain Tijen of the Splosna Plovba line. He and the lifeboat crew were recommended for the Yugoslav Blue Ribbon, awarded for outstanding services at sea. The crew of the *Integrity* were landed in Bermuda and were compensated and repatriated by Integrity Charters Inc. The *Integrity* herself remained in the ocean. For her the fight was not over—she had in her that quality of tough, stubborn determination known in humans as grit. Those who have it, whether people or boats, are the hangers-on, the survivors who battle through against the odds. The *Integrity* survived the lubbers—now she was to fall among thieves.

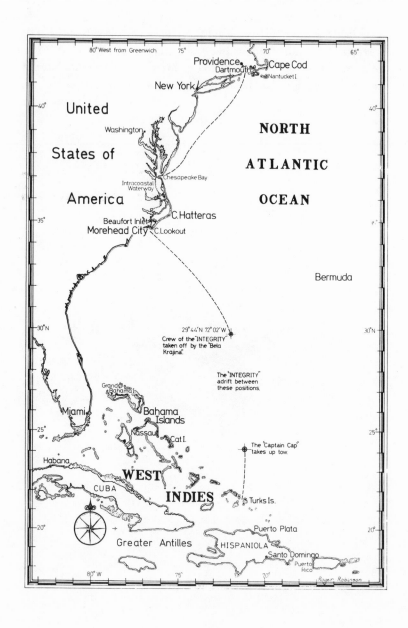

80° West from Greenwich   75°   70°   65°

Providence
Dartmouth
New York
Cape Cod
Nantucket I.

United

NORTH

40°

Washington

States of

ATLANTIC

Chesapeake Bay

America

OCEAN

35°

Intracoastal
Waterway
C. Hatteras
Beaufort Inlet
Morehead City   C. Lookout

Bermuda

30° N

29°44'N 72°02'W

Crew of the "INTEGRITY"
taken off by the "Bela
Krajina".

The "INTEGRITY"
adrift between
these positions.

Grand
Bahama

Bahama
Islands

Miami

The "Captain Cap"
takes up tow.

25°

Nassau   Cat I.

Habana

WEST

CUBA

INDIES

Turks Is.

20°

Puerto Plata

Greater Antilles
HISPANIOLA
Santo Domingo
Puerto
Rico

80° W   75°   70°   Roger Robinson

CHAPTER VIII

If the *Integrity* had been any ordinary vessel this story
would now be at an end. She had lived through her span of
life, although a short one, not without credit. She had made a
distinguished voyage across the Atlantic to England and
Portugal, she had made another voyage, almost as commend-
able, from Dartmouth, Massachusetts to Grenada in the far
south of the Caribbean. She had proved Waldo's point and she
had fulfilled his ambition. It was true, the old schooners of the
coast, with all their traditions, with all the lore and wisdom
that had been put into their construction, had marked a
zenith in the design and building of sailing vessels. The
Integrity proved it. Waldo knew it and when he stood astride
her poop and felt the thrill of her movement, he was aware
that he had recreated a thing of beauty. The *Integrity*,
through Waldo, became famous among yachtsmen and seamen up and down the eastern seaboard of the United States
and much further afield. Old hands looked up and nodded
their heads wisely when she came into a harbour. She became
more famous than her builder or than any person who ever
had dealings with her. She was not well known because of
Waldo—rather it was her glory which reflected on him and this
was the greatest tribute she received. Being a thoroughbred

79

in spirit as well as in her breeding, she fought hardest when things were most against her and being a belle of fame she could always be relied on to do the unexpected. Her delivery crew, on board the *Bela Krajina* bound for Bermuda, regarded her as dead and gone. Perhaps it would have been better if she had been dead and gone—Frank West told me that afterwards the crew cursed themselves for not making certain that she sank before they left her.

Nobody knows the full story of the experiences of the *Integrity* lived through for the next month. There were sightings, reports of positions, rumours of towings, vague stories of boardings. What is certain is that when Geoffrey Innes's yacht *Captain Cap* came across her she had been ravished. It is a fact that otherwise honest and upright men at once lose every vestige of their morality when they see the wreck of a boat, a ship or even a house. There is some psychological reaction which, when he sees the fabric of someone else's life in ruins, makes a man throw principles to the winds and plunge in to rape and plunder. He will come away with the loot under his arm and with no feeling of guilt or even the awareness that he has done anything amiss. I knew a man whose boat was cast up on some beach—he went for assistance and came back to find a line of people departing with his belongings. They were mildly offended when he asked for his things back. The *Integrity* was plundered during her month of wandering with a sort of haphazard thoroughness. The food in her lockers had been stripped out of her—not a can was left. Even the can opener had been unscrewed from the bulkhead. Plates, bowls, cups, mugs were all gone, the racks in the galley empty. The homely pictures in the main cabin and the owners' cabin had been taken, the Loran navigation receiver had gone as had the radio and the compass. Yet a portable generator had been left, a new air horn, expensive tools, new canvas and rope, anchors, bronze blocks. There had been some apparently wanton smashing of the nicely carpentered cabin fittings.

After the *Bela Krajina's* message nothing was seen of the *Integrity* for six days when she was sighted by a container ship, the *M/V Floridian.* She radioed the U.S. Coastguard that the yacht was dismasted, her life raft missing and no one on board. A yacht called the *Colette* was in contact with the *Floridian* but nothing is known of her or her crew. Next the *Integrity* was seen by the *Alcaid,* a tanker bound for New York from Trinidad. She gave the Coastguard another position and reported that a party had gone aboard but had found no persons and no log book. The schooner, the *Alcaid* reported, was a danger to navigation. Next the Coastguard received a letter from Captain Milton L. Jones, a marine surveyor of Miami who gave two positions for the *Integrity* with an unspecified period of time between them and suggested that she was drifting towards the south. According to Captain Jones a tanker, the *Atlantic Queen* and a Swedish ship, the *Sonette,* had both put lines on board the yacht and had tried to tow her but had both been forced to abandon their attempts because of bad weather. Between the *Bela Krajina* on November 6th and the *Captain Cap* on December 1st four positions are given for the *Integrity* from these sources. They show that the yacht drifted SSE at 20 miles a day except for the period between the sightings by the *Floridian* and the *Alcaid* when she drifted in the opposite direction at 8 miles per day and between the *Alcaid* and Captain Jones's first position when she made to the west at 15 miles a day. This tallies with the current in that part of the ocean in November which flows weakly towards the west and with a southerly going current which was logged by the *Captain Cap.* It also fits with the prevailing wind which is N to NE. In normal conditions she would drift on a southerly course but if it blew from the west as it sometimes does, briefly, she would drift more slowly eastwards.

The *Captain Cap* was a fine old ship—a ship that Waldo himself would have admired. She was originally a trawler built in 1910 by a Scotsman called Stoba in the Fleetwood yard of James Armour and Sons. One of her sister ships, but slightly smaller, was the *Reliance,* heroine of Ann Davison's sad and brilliant book *Last Voyage. Captain Cap* was 68 feet long on the water line—a very large and immensely heavy ship. She was massively built—Geoffrey Innes told me her planking was of 3 inch teak, thickening to 4½ inches at the turn of the bilge but that she had been repaired at various times with pitch pine. Her frames and her main timbers were all of oak, her stringers, which run the whole length of the ship inside the frames, were 22 inches wide and 5 inches thick. Like the *Reliance,* when she was converted to a yacht her rig had been cut down—she lost her fine gaff main and mizzen and was given "leg of mutton" sails in their place—a sad but all too common fate. Her sail area had been cut in half although she had been spared her bowsprit, a fine spar projecting 17 foot over the stem. Her overall length from the tip of the bowsprit to the end of the mizzen boom was 104 feet. She had a splendid diesel engine—a Gardner 6 L.W. which had been put in her in 1958 and which, if pushed, could drive her at over 8 knots. At the beginning of her life, long before the engine had been put in, she had worked with the Brixham trawler fleet. As she had been an exceptionally fast sailer she had been used as a "runner" to take the fleet's catch to port while they kept the sea. As a yacht she belonged to another age. The massiveness of her construction, her sheer size must have made her a very expensive headache. The cost of slipping her and painting her, even the cost of mooring her alongside a quay, would make an ordinary yachtsman turn pale.

I have never met Geoffrey Innes although he has corresponded with me at great length. His letters to me have contained a flood of information, written in a tiny, close hand in immaculate English. I first got his address from the Lloyd's Register of Yachts—it was a forwarding address, a Bank in a suburb of London. Months passed before his first letter came from the West Indies and later, when we got to know each other better through our correspondence, he wrote to me copiously from Australia, sending me extracts from the *Captain Cap's* log and pages of beautifully written description.

Captain Cap was on passage from Nassau to the Leeward

Islands. She had on board a crew of seven including Geoffrey Innes and his wife. One of them, Les Hummel, was a paid hand—he is described by Geoffrey Innes as "delivery first mate" and, in the *Yachting Magazine* article as "delivery Captain." Perhaps Geoffrey Innes employed Hummel because he wanted a professional yacht hand to stiffen his crew of amateurs and to relieve him of some of the responsibility. Hummel had been recommended by a friend but the arrangement was not a success from the beginning. Innes's wife Edythe disliked him, describing him as an "ugly American"— she was an American herself—by which she meant his nature, not his looks. Geoffrey Innes thought he was something of an "Errol Flynn", a poseur, a complex character who always found it necessary to impress his personality on the crew— perhaps by giving them unnecessary work to do or by exerting his" authority whenever the occasion presented itself. He had a desire for recognition and publicity and he saw dollar signs floating in the air in front of his eyes. *Captain Cap* had been at sea for four days when, at noon on December 1st, she came on the *Integrity* wallowing in the swell. She was seen by Lou Le Huray, a Guernseyman, who was at the wheel. An immediate and infectious excitement spread through the ship. They all crowded on deck, all clamoured impatiently for the binoculars. As the *Captain Cap* drew near it became clear that they had stumbled upon a disaster. Shouts, whistles and foghorns produced no response from the *Integrity*. She rolled in the ocean swell, detached, silent and disinterested, her broken spars and gear still strewn about her deck and in the water beside her. It was as if she wanted no further dealings with any human hand. Geoffrey Innes read her name through the binoculars and at once, with a tight feeling in his throat, he realised that it was the *Integrity* he knew well. He said the sight of her brought tears to his eyes. He had first seen her in Grenada, had met Waldo several times and had corresponded with him, although Waldo himself does not remember this. *Captain Cap's* mainsail was lowered and she lost way.

Geoffrey Innes decided that the *Integrity* should be boarded. There was too much clutter in the sea for *Captain Cap* to be put alongside, there was too much swell to lower a boat—someone would have to swim. Hummel volunteered. Innes was dubious—he knew Hummel had been involved in a motor accident only a few months before—but finally he agreed. The *Captain Cap* was brought to within a few yards of the derelict and Hummel dived over. He had some difficulty in swimming the distance in the ocean swell—he was in poor physical condition. Although he was still a young man he had led a soft life in the pursuit of business and in running a Miami art gallery. It was not easy to get on board. He swam round the schooner, searching for a way up her smooth, green sides until he came to the folds of the mainsail, half over the side and half on deck. He was able to gain a foothold and climb on board. He shouted, looked below and then hailed the *Captain Cap*. There was no-one on board.

He was able to gain a foothold and climb on board.

The story of Hummel boarding the *Integrity* is told by a lady journalist in *Yachting Magazine*. She seems to have caught a part of Hummel's romantic and melodramatic air and to have cast him correctly in his role.

"What are your intentions?" Geoffrey Innes, the trawler's British owner asked Hummel. The skipper's light blue eyes squinted across at the derelict and he folded his lips tightly in his full chestnut beard.

"I intend to board her", he said. Then he swung himself up the ratlines to take a look for sharks.

The cobalt waters of the Atlantic glinted back, innocent of treacherous dark shadows. Hummel dropped back on deck and stripped down to shorts and tee shirt. He left on his sneakers, explaining "Sharks make a pass at your toes. If they scrape and draw blood, they come back."

Shortly after Hummel swam over he was joined by another member of the *Captain Cap's* crew, Harry Hess. They found the schooner's decks knee-deep in a perplexing litter of junk and mess. Broken glass was everywhere, mattresses and bedding had been dragged up from below and left all over the deck. Broken plates, cutlery and kitchen gear clogged the scuppers, engine room tools lay scattered haphazardly, one of the bilge pumps, its handle bent almost double, rolled back and forth with the yacht's motion. They could discern efforts to make up some rudimentary form of towing gear— lengths of wire which had been crudely made into strops, rope of several different sizes fastened like a cat's cradle round the windlass and the stump of the foremast.

Through the open hatches they heard strange sounds from below. Doors banged to and fro as the *Integrity* rolled, her timbers seemed to creak eerily, loose gear slid from side to side. But she was dry—the bilge water was only up to the cabin sole. They went below with trepidation, half expecting to find tangible evidence of disaster—a dead man, the signs of violence or of some evil treachery. There was nothing but the same disorder that was apparent on deck but overlaid by the stench of sickness, stale urine and rotting excreta. They could see at once that she had been looted—perhaps several times. Drawers were pulled out and overturned, lockers were empty, left with their doors swinging, bunk mattresses had been thrown haphazardly to one side and the spaces beneath crudely broken open. They noted the battery box still jammed upside down behind the engine. The engine appeared to be undamaged—the flywheel could be turned by hand but without power there was no means of starting it.

There were signs that the *Integrity* had been under tow. Lengths of rope of sizes and qualities that no yacht would carry were fastened to the rails and stanchions apparently in an attempt to make a bridle. There was a strop of one-inch steel wire, odd pieces of braided manilla and a length of polypropylene hawser had been knotted round deck fittings and pulled tight as if under tremendous strain. The anchor windlass had been wrenched askew on its fastenings. The decks were strewn with broken spars, oddments of rope and wire, pieces of clothing, empty tins, torn sails and fenders, as well as the broken glass. When Hummel and Hess had looked over the yacht and made preparations for connecting the tow, Innes brought the *Captain Cap* close and a line was passed—a new piece of 1 inch nylon 300 feet long. Two hours after the *Integrity* had been sighted she was securely fast astern of the *Captain Cap* and on her way to the island of Grand Turk, 150 miles to the south.

With remarkable patience and good sense Geoffrey Innes towed the *Integrity* under sail, without using the *Captain Cap's* excellent engine until the last few miles when he was approaching the anchorage in Grand Turk. Presumably he wanted to save his fuel and clearly he knew that he was more likely to succeed if he towed slowly. The cardinal mistake, invariably made when a more powerful vessel is towing a yacht, is to go too fast. Innes could see that the *Integrity* was damaged and he knew that he would aggravate this damage, possibly make her unseaworthy, if he imposed heavy strains on her. As it happened the *Captain Cap,* with her great weight and stability, made an excellent tug. She had, after all, spent the first twenty-five years of her life as a trawler and was designed to pull heavy gear. She was fitted with a fine U-shaped transit timber on her fan-tail grating aft, of massive build and amply through bolted to the ship's frames which made an excellent towing horse. Because she was so large and heavy she had no difficulty in steering with the dead weight of the *Integrity* hanging behind her but chafe was a problem. Even at slow speed the nylon tow line tended to work backwards and forwards through the fair lead by its own elasticity so that it heated itself by friction. It was frequently necessary to lengthen or shorten the tow by a few fathoms.

A messenger line was improvised so that supplies could be passed across the sea from tug to tow in a large plastic ice chest, wrapped in plastic bags and sealed with tape. In this way some food was passed across—the bread arrived wet—a few necessary tools, sleeping bags, blankets and clothing for Hummel and Hess. Hummel particularly asked for a chart, which was sent across on the messenger. Their first job was to cut adrift the mast and sails. It was not difficult. Hummel, with great good seamanship, had provided himself with a heavy serrated edge knife which had been passed over in the ice box. The lanyards on both masts were easily cut through and once the mast hoops had been cut from the mainsail and the sheets freed, most of the fear floated free. The mainsail itself they dragged back on board. The broken bowsprit and jib-boom was more difficult—it was held by a dozen stays and lines which were either undone or cut. A message from Hummel to the *Captain Cap* describes this work graphically. "Log this", it begins imperiously. "1. We have unbolted and cut away bowsprit. 2. Cut away wreckage of the mast over side. 3. Gotten parts of spars and sail back in boat—swam in water in the face of sharks. 4. Removed steering cover, cut away old cable. 5. Removed wreckage to get below. 6. Made temporary waterproof patches. 7. Note: boat has been previously looted."

Geoffrey Innes thought the bow planking might have been

damaged by the vicious battering of the broken 'sprit—but this was not so. Once freed of the web of gear that had held her, the *Integrity* towed easily, taking station on the *Captain Cap's* port quarter. What water there was in the bilge was quickly disposed of by the deck pumps. Her steering gear was repaired with a coil of spare rope which Hummel found in the store. Tired by an afternoon of excitement and hard work, the two men turned in to sleep in all the filth and stench below decks, taking watch and watch through the night. At daybreak they started work at once—cleaning out the accommodation throwing overboard filthy bedding and pillows and swilling down with water. It is not clear how the *Integrity* got into such a mess below decks. I thought at first that it must have been left by a hopelessly seasick and demoralised crew but I found out from Frank West that this was not so. The crew were demoralised after the knockdown— by the labour of steering with a jury rig and by the general feeling of hopeless disorder, but they had not been sick. If they had been, certainly not indiscriminately. It must have been one of several of the boarding parties who were responsible for the filth. Coming from a big ship to a small one they would have found the motion violent enough to make them ill very quickly and not knowing the *Integrity,* they might not have been considerate of her. After cleaning broken glass and splinters of wood and metal from the decks, Hummel improved the yacht's trim, bringing her head up by shifting aft some of the finely cut granite blocks that had been used as ballast. Some of these blocks, curiously enough, had been looted and two or three, like the one that had destroyed Peter's bunk, had broken out from the bilges. But it was impossible to see whether the ballast had shifted seriously. Geoffrey Innes told me that the blocks were not properly wedged in position and could well have come free, but there was no bilge-water mark on the white cabin sides to show how far she had gone over in the knock-down.

Now that the schooner was fairly in tow, Hummel and Hess got sail on her. The stump of main mast was still slippery with Captain Culler's patent stikkum and defied Hummel's efforts to climb it, but ingeniously, he fastened steps to the mast which he cut from odd pieces of dunnage he found on board, nailing on a step at a time as he went up. It was no mean feat to gain the top of the mast, fasten two blocks with a strop and rig halliards. He found a sail for the after part of his rig—it may have been part of the *Integrity's* fisherman, or a genoa or even a spinnaker—and he hacked to pieces one of the beautiful tan-barked sails to make the for'ard part. As soon as she had sail up the motion eased and life became bearable. The wind was light and fair and the speed of the little convoy increased slightly. But there was no hurry—Geoffrey Innes knew that they could not reach Turks before nightfall on December 3rd.

On the evening of December 2nd the weather took a sudden turn for the worse—a small and intense depression. These patches of unsettled weather are frequent in this part of the Bahamas in the winter—they are unheralded by any forecast and come up suddenly out of a fine sky. The wind swings to the north and blows hard, perhaps as hard as Force 7, for two or three hours, kicking up a heavy chop over the long swell, then the whole thing evaporates and in a few hours butter wouldn't melt in the weather's mouth. Innes had anticipated bad weather. In a message to Hummel sent over the line, he said:

"Here is a marked chart. . . with pencils and instruments. Your course is south to Turks Islands. . . If weather gets bad we will come up on your lee, to take you and Harry off if necessary, abandoning the tow, but standing by to resume it when conditions become favourable. . . At all costs, hang on to your end of the messenger line. Well done! Good luck! and Good night!"

The bad weather came suddenly. The sky clouded over very quickly, a small, compact black cloud formed up to windward and came rapidly towards them. The wind swung round to the north and in minutes it was blowing hard. The

89

squall caught the *Captain Cap* with her mainsail up and all hands were called out to get it in as quickly as possible. She began to roll heavily, the shift of wind putting her across the swell and it was all they could do to get the immensely heavy main boom secured. The *Integrity* rolled even more heavily, up to 45° either side, but the tow line held. Within two hours the blow was over and the weather returned to its normal pattern.

In the night a freighter passed close astern of the tow but didn't see them. The next day they were spoken by a tug towing a barge which circled round, came close to the *Integrity*, passed over some provisions and asked if help was needed. "Looks like you guys got there ahead of me," the tug skipper shouted across to Hummel ruefully. Geoffrey Innes tried to relay a message to Lloyd's and to the U.S. Coastguard through the tug skipper but communications were difficult. The tug, with its barge in tow, came close alongside the *Integrity* but could not approach the *Captain Cap* for fear of fouling the tow line. Geoffrey shouted a signal across but it was never sent. Instead, Hummel, being close alongside, relayed his own message through the tug. He later told Geoffrey that he had sent messages to the U.S. Coastguard and various of his own friends in Miami, including the Miami Herald, telling them about the *Integrity's* rescue.

Later in the day, Hummel sent a message over on the line.

"We have taken a lot of weight off the tow line with the sail. Expect to be able to sail into harbour when the other sail is rigged. . . we have lost track of time. What day of the week is this—incredible motion—exhausting. . ."

Already nerves were beginning to fray and relations between Geoffrey Innes and Hummel were beginning to deteriorate. I believe the two men had almost opposite characters— Geoffrey meticulous, pedantic, cautious, nervous, sensitive and Hummel brash, bombastic, conceited, arrogant, opportunist. Nonetheless in some ways he must have been a likeable character—he was a good improviser and a good

90

seaman as Geoffrey Innes would admit readily. He had lots of nerve. From this moment their conflicting personalities worked against each other. Geoffrey Innes replied to Hummel's message,

> "There is no harbour at Grand Turk. . . the 10-fathom line is about 1½ cables off shore, then shoals dangerously and suddenly about 100 yards off shore. Therefore, there is no question of sailing *Integrity* in and you will not do so. *Captain Cap* will tow *Integrity* in. . . Thank you for the hard work you and Harry have put in. . ."

There was a last excitement on this last night of the tow when Hummel shouted across to the *Captain Cap,* having gauged the tow's course from the North Star, "You are sailing an untenable course—reef dead ahead." The *Captain Cap's* helmsman, catching a note of panic in Hummel's voice, "altered course aimlessly", but radio bearings were taken to check the D.R. position and in less than an hour, as predicted, the loom of the light on the north of Grand Turk was raised. The convoy turned into the Turks Islands Passage between Turks and Caicos. At daylight the *Captain Cap's* engine was started, the tow's jury sails were taken down and she turned into the wind and tugged against it, making slow progress until midday when she was within three miles of the anchorage off Grand Turk. It was then that Les Hummel slipped the tow, turned the *Integrity's* head to starboard, hoisted his jury sails and made off towards a haven of his own in Cockburn Town, South Caicos. It was the first overt action in a long campaign of greed and chicanery that bedevilled the *Integrity* from that moment until her final demise.

The *Integrity* in tow of *Captain Cap*.

Bill set one of *Iskra's* spare sails on the stump of *Integrity's* mast.

Even in a light breeze, *Iskra* towed *Integrity* at a brisk 2½ knots.

Paul steers *Iskra* with *Integrity* in tow.

CHAPTER IX

From what I know of Geoffrey Innes I doubt whether the question of salvage was uppermost in his mind when he saw the *Integrity* adrift in the ocean and decided to take her in tow. More likely he recognised in the *Integrity* value for its own sake—something unusual, even unique, a thing of worth and beauty crying to be rescued. Certainly the sight of a derelict or of a vessel in distress and wanting assistance strikes a chord in the hearts of most seamen, whether it be of sentiment or the sniff of salvage. Sailorizing is a hard life and the prospect of a quick and lucky return for a small effort is enough to make any salty tongue curl round its own lips. I remember from my own experience in ocean tugs that it was the prospect and occasionally the reality of salvage that sustained us through the weeks and months of cold and discomfort. Most sailors, even those who have had no experience in tugs, nourish a dream deep inside themselves that one day in their wanderings across the world's oceans they will come up with a prize of such immense value that it will keep them in idle luxury for the rest of their natural lives. The laws governing salvage have evolved over hundreds of years of seafaring and are purposely weighted in favour of the man who is prepared to risk his time, his money, even his life to drag a cripple in from the sea. It can be a very profitable business. On the other hand, for saving life at sea there is no reward except in the knowledge of a deed well done. The laws vary from country to country as does the proportion of the salvage award that is paid to each member of the crew. An Admiralty court will take many factors into account—the risk taken, the skill and seamanship displayed, weather and sea conditions, the amount of time taken, the degree of enterprise shown. Geoffrey Innes must have assumed that there would be no difficulty about the *Integrity's* salvage claim—it was a straightforward case of valuable property saved from the sea. It was clear that he had carried out the salvage with complete success although with difficulty and at some expense, if not danger to himself and his own people. There can have been no doubt in his mind that a fair salvage claim would be paid as a matter of course.

The whole thing, he must have assumed, would be settled in an amicable way between himself and the *Integrity's* insurance company without recourse to the law and that the proceeds would be divided among the *Captain Cap's* crew in whatever was the usual and proper proportion. Presumably he decided to take the *Integrity* to Grand Turk because it was the nearest suitable haven, because it was on his way and because he believed that being a British island, he would be on his home ground and more certain to get a fair deal. It was something over 150 miles from where he picked up the *Integrity* to Grand Turk, it was about 330 miles to Nassau and a further 160 miles to Miami. If he had known then what he was to learn, little by little over the eight weeks that the *Captain Cap* spent in Turks Island, he would most probably have towed the *Integrity* all the way to Miami—or perhaps he would have left her where he found her in the ocean.

There is no doubt that salvage was uppermost in Les Hummel's mind. In his first message from the *Integrity* he mentioned it. "We are working like Hell—the insurance company will want her at a good price—how about half for the six crew Captain—that's only fair—you must make a report in the log that you endangered your vessel repeatedly and seriously to make the salvage, to strengthen your claim. Include in your notes that I am a master carpenter, boat builder and rigger. It will look good to a maritime court. Log this—." Relations between Innes and Hummel deteriorated rapidly. Hummel seems to have considered himself to be in charge of the whole operation. His messages across to the *Captain Cap,* in a bold, crude hand seemed to have all been written with an eye to the insurance claim. "Mr. Innes, my question is, if you receive funds for salvage—may we share in that amount?" The next message reads, "This is dangerous enough at sea to merit a share, never mind the incredible work", and soon afterwards, "It is customary to work salvage at one-third for crew, one-third master, one-third owner. Will you abide by this—if not what deal?"

Geoffrey Innes replied somewhat curtly,

"Your notes will go into the log complete, as they stand. As for salvage, British procedure will be followed. I do not know what this is in detail, but there is a standard practice and there is a proper official (maybe an Admiralty Marshal) to hand *Integrity* over to."

As the article in *Yachting Magazine* put it, "the. . . camaraderie that had existed prior to the sighting of *Integrity* disappeared in a sickening atmosphere of suspicion, secretiveness and hostility."

Apart from writing notes and sending them across on the messenger line, Hummel and Hess worked doggedly, in spite of the rolling and the appalling conditions on board. The other members of the *Captain Cap's* crew accepted Geoffrey Innes's word about the salvage claim without question. There was acrimony about sailing the *Integrity* into harbour and about *Captain Cap's* allegedly zig-zag course. When Hummel slipped the tow off the anchorage, set sail and made off in the direction of South Caicos on the opposite side of the Turks Islands Passage, there was only one thing for Innes to do. He made anchorage in Grand Turk as soon as he could, went straight ashore and at once contacted the Chief of Police and

95

the Harbour Master. He explained the circumstances and asked for a maritime lien to be put on the *Integrity*, whereupon a launch was immediately got ready and Innes, together with a police escort, put to sea, boarded the *Integrity* and towed her to the Turks anchorage under arrest. They found her already in tow of a fisherman in a small boat powered by an outboard engine to whom Hummel had offered ten dollars for a tow into South Caicos. He had hoisted an American flag made out of a tee shirt and was bound as hell for leather as he could, for Cockburn Town. He may have thought that the *Captain Cap* could not follow because of her draft. If he had arrived there he would no doubt have made his own salvage claim and the subsequent confusion would have been further complicated.

There was a tense moment on the *Integrity's* deck when the police boarded her. Hummel was at the wheel, although the wind had fallen light and the schooner was hardly moving. He refused to obey when the Chief of Police ordered him to hand over the wheel to a police sergeant. Two burly constables moved quietly behind him—their hands were raised to put a half nelson on him and remove him below when his resistance caved. He was arrested and Hess was arrested with him but was released when he offered to help berth the schooner. Hummel was kept under arrest, although his freedom was not restricted, until he left the island on December 11th. No charge was ever proffered against him.

What Geoffrey Innes did not know and what Les Hummel did not know and what neither of them guessed, was that the *Integrity* was no longer the responsibility of any insurance company. Soon after the news came from the *Bela Krajina* that she was adrift, derelict in the ocean, the insurance company paid out a total loss claim. In this way the insurance company washed its hands of the whole affair and ownership of the *Integrity*, or what was left of her, rested with Integrity Charters Inc. together with the responsibility for any claim against her. The owners wanted the *Integrity* back—with her name, her background and her recent adventures behind her she would still be a valuable asset—but, understandably, they were not over anxious to pay out a large salvage claim. Accordingly, as soon as they had successfully completed their negotiations with the insurance company, they set about the task of finding the derelict for themselves. When the *Captain Cap* arrived in Grand Turk, a Miami marine surveyor, the same Milton L. Jones who had already reported the *Integrity's* position a few weeks previously, was preparing to carry out a search for her. As the *Integrity* was drifting in a part of the Bermuda Triangle which is criss-crossed by yachts and shipping routes, a sighting was more than likely. Equally it was not likely that any ship would consider it worth while, or even feasible, to tow the *Integrity* in and not likely that any yacht could do so. Jones's plan was to wait for a sighting, then to send out an aircraft to pin-point the derelict and then to commission a suitable motor boat to pick her up, guided to the spot by the aircraft. Jones, as it happened, was familiar with that part of the Bahamas. He may have known a certain Ron Bamber, the owner of an expensive hotel on Cat Island, 300 miles to the north west of Turks and opposite the spot where the *Integrity* might well show up according to the reported positions. It also happened that Bamber was the owner of a light aircraft which he used to flit back and forth to Miami, Nassau and Freeport in connection with his hotel business—and it happened that Bamber was interested in buying the *Integrity* so that she could lie at anchor off the hotel and take his guests for day sails and short cruises. She would add a note of great distinction to a hotel—she would be something very exclusive.

Milton L. Jones was therefore a very surprised man when he heard that the *Integrity* had appeared in Turks astern of the *Captain Cap*. Innes told me he had refused to believe it until he saw it with his own eyes. Indeed, the old *Captain Cap* with her heavy displacement and her steadiness was a vessel well suited for towing a derelict for over 150 miles—most modern yachts would not have undertaken it. When she arrived in Grand Turk the *Integrity* was turned over to the

Receiver of Wrecks, Innes retaining a lien on her himself—and there she stayed while the sluggish wheels of bureaucracy were coaxed into a dull and lethargic activity and while Geoffrey Innes strove to unravel the tangle of personalities that lay between him and a settlement of his claim for salvage. His crew, including a disconsolate Hummel, melted away in pursuit of their various activities while he and his wife and a couple of hands that remained, looked after the *Integrity*, moved her from the open anchorage into the Hawk's Nest, made repairs as best they could and kept the yacht pumped out.

Turks and Caicos, being British Crown colonies, in fact made it more difficult for Innes's claim. The *Integrity's* owners were Americans and even if a salvage claim had been speedily adjudicated in Turks it would not have been binding on them without further legal action. The mere fact that the *Integrity* was in Turks at all, decreased her value enormously. Although her hull was sound, before she could be made once more into a yacht she would need a substantial sum of money spending on her in a proper yard—a surveyor who looked at her in Turks estimated it at 20,000 dollars. This would entail, at the start, a long and very expensive tow. The owners wanted the *Integrity* back but they did not wish to pay out a full salvage claim. Innes told me that under U.S. maritime law, if a yacht is not claimed by her owner she can be considered as of no value to him and he cannot be made to pay for her salvage.

The first thing that Hummel did when he was landed in Turks Islands and released from close police custody was to contact Miami. Later he told Innes to expect an immediate American invasion. Two days later the marine surveyor Milton L. Jones arrived in Turks Islands accompanied by a lawyer called Martin Goode. They came in a specially chartered aeroplane. Jones was the best known marine surveyor in Miami and it would have been natural for Hummel to have contacted him. He was also well known to Geoffrey Innes—the lawyer represented the *Integrity's* owners.

98

The two of them arrived on December 9th. Innes didn't much like the lawyer—he described him to me as a "suave whizz-kid" and said he was wary of him. Jones inspected the *Integrity* but Goode, seeing the way she rolled in the anchorage, decided that his duty as a lawyer did not require him actually to go on board. There was a long and confused meeting between Jones, Goode, Innes, Hummel and several others of the crew at which some attempt was made to settle a claim.

They all came together in the hotel. Goode settled himself comfortably on a settee in the alcove of the bar "like a man of the world faced by a lot of simpletons." Astonishingly to Innes, he opened the discussion by asking whether he, Innes, would like to buy the *Integrity* as she was, for $3,000. Innes declined, saying that he already had one boat which was enough. Goode then offered $3,000 as the salvage award—a sum which was met with derision by everybody present. Even Jones pressed Goode to raise the figure to $4,000 but he refused. Feelings ran high, everyone present put in his word but Goode remained firm and eventually, seeing no prospect of agreement, closed the meeting. He and Jones settled down to lunch before leaving for the return flight to Miami.

Geoffrey Innes, at least temporarily burying his differences with Hummel, got together with the others and tried to work out an acceptable figure. After covering several sheets of paper with figures they came up with the sum of $10,500 which, although they considered it quite inadequate, they all reluctantly agreed to accept. However, Goode, knowing perfectly well that he was on unshakeable ground because of the question of jurisdiction, rejected this flatly. Hummel, who by this time was in a towering rage, picked up the papers, stuffed them into his pocket and walked out, so ending the discussion. It was the nearest Geoffrey Innes ever got to a settlement.

It was not easy for Innes to discover his exact legal position in this remote spot. There was one lawyer on the island, whom he had engaged, but neither he nor Innes was an expert on maritime law. Turks apparently has its own laws which differ from the law of England in such a way that Innes could not get legal ownership of the *Integrity,* or transfer the whole case to England. Therefore when Bamber eventually contacted him and made him an offer for the yacht, Innes could not accept because he only had a lien on her which did not entitle him to sell. The transaction could have been arranged through the owners but according to Innes they would not make the sale possible by using Bamber's purchase price to settle the salvage claim. They still hoped to get the *Integrity* for themselves, for nothing or for a small sum. Innes had another offer for the yacht which he turned down for the same reason. The confusion was confounded because Innes could not find out who the owners were—it was a long time before he identified them. A firm of maritime lawyers from Miami who represented the owners and the insurance company sent a man to Turks but he would not tell Innes who the owners were. Innes then wrote to Waldo and asked him but received an evasive reply. There seems to have been a general feeling of mistrust on all sides—accusations and counter-accusations flew like grape shot. In the meantime the owners, Integrity Charters Inc. used the insurance money to buy another yacht which they renamed *Free Spirit.*

The *Captain Cap* spent eight weeks in Turks Islands—she did not leave until it became certain that nothing was to be settled quickly and possible that nothing would ever be settled. Innes left the local lawyer in charge of his affairs and the *Integrity* in charge of the Receiver of Wrecks in Turks Islands, swinging gently and pensively to her mooring in Hawk's Nest and wondering what the fates or the dispositions of man would have in store for her next. It is hard to understand why at this juncture, Innes did not repair the *Integrity's* engines and take her to Miami under her own power. It is hard to believe that even with the limited resources of Turks Islands, it would have been impossible to get the engine going. It was a very good engine and a very reliable one. The *Integrity* could have been in Miami within days and in a far stronger position to negotiate salvage. I can only believe that there may have been some legal impediment to this course of action. The *Captain Cap* went on her way to Antigua and the Windward Islands—as she went she found that the story of the *Integrity* had gone before her in one form or another. Geoffrey Innes discovered the names of the owners, discovered that they had already spent their gains on another yacht and were therefore unlikely ever to pay a salvage claim unless forced to do so by the law. He discovered that one of the three owners had visited Turks, had inspected the *Integrity* and had been anxious to settle the salvage claim but had been unable to carry his two partners with him.

The Supreme Court, Admiralty Division, met in Grand Turk over a year later but it seemed as if they had come together only to preside over more and more delays and extensions. First the judge resigned then another judge was appointed who in his turn resigned. The British Colonial Supreme Court, with all the powers of the Supreme Court of England, made haste slowly, at every turn running foul of procedure and precedent with the accumulated mountain of Admiralty and Colonial jurisprudence at its disposal. Predictably, the deliberations of this body were inconclusive. Time dragged remorselessly on, with every passing month and year the probability of any satisfactory settlement became more and more remote. Incredibly, the case file containing the only record of the court proceedings was inexplicably lost and the court never gave a written judgment, thus rendering its conclusions valueless in any foreign jurisdiction. No tangible reward for their labours, to Innes, Hummel or his crew ever came out of it. Finally, on June 13th, 1973, the unprofitable legal charade having stumbled to a halt, the weathered and battered hull of the *Integrity,* after swinging to her lines for three and a half years, a prey to deterioration of every kind—sun, wind, rain and rot as well as the depredations of casual marauders, was put up for auction in Grand Turk. By this time Geoffrey Innes told me the affair, including his legal costs, had cost him more than 30,000

101

dollars of which sum no single penny ever returned to him. On the very day the auction was to have taken place, the very 13th of June, 1973, the schooner was found sunk at her moorings—lying on the sand bottom in no more than twelve feet of water, every detail of her hull clearly visible from above through the translucent Bahamian ocean.

Her hull clearly visible from above the
translucent Bahamian ocean.

CHAPTER X

It is hard to see how Bill could have hoped to make the boatyard into a profitable business venture. I don't know whether the nucleus of the miscellaneous huts and sheds and lean-to stores was there before he came, or whether he constructed them himself. Bill was an industrious soul and the place had an air of purpose and optimism which belied the emptiness of its surroundings. It was a boatyard with no boats—except a few tenders and fishing boats which belonged to Bill and of course, the *Integrity*. She had been there, sometimes on the bottom and sometimes afloat, since before Bill. The island, at that time, hoped and expected that it was on the edge of a tourist boom that would transform its lagging and torpid economy. Soon hotels would be built and rich people from America would come to adorn the inexhaustible beaches and to spend their money on all manner of delights. Bill's boatyard would be right in at the beginning. It hadn't worked out like that. The tourists, as sometimes happens, had gone elsewhere. The boatyard was three miles outside the sleepy, hot little town where the only life of the island flourished, along the dusty winding track through the unworked salt pans. No one ever came there except Bill on his old motor bike without a silencer. Chauncey and Heather had their business enterprise on a surer foundation with their tropical fish export business as bread and butter and a diving school as the occasional cream. Apart from Heather's business, Chauncey had his work at the NASA base.

Geoffrey Innes never went back to Turks after he left with the *Captain Cap*. He told me he had flown over the island one bright day and had looked down on the *Integrity*. She was on the bottom of the Hawk's Nest anchorage at the time under twelve feet of water. The sea was so clear that he could see every detail of her—it had been hard to believe that she was not afloat. In spite of the disappointments and financial loss he had suffered at her hands he felt a stab of nostalgia for the schooner as the aeroplane flew past. It was remarkable how she was able to exert a fascination over those who were thrown into contact with her. From her conception to her end she possessed a charisma of her own which few people were unaffected by. When Bill had first told me about her and when I first saw her she was simply a hulk—of passing interest perhaps but essentially a characterless and even slightly ludicrous piece of decaying boat. The thought that anyone could have the incentive to do anything constructive with her was ridiculous. Later, when I came to know her, she was to communicate to me something of her character and in the end I became committed to her and embroiled to the hilt in her fortunes.

After she sank on the day she was to be sold by auction she lay on the bottom for many months. She was photographed by a Canadian visitor to Turks and later, the ghostly underwater pictures were published in *Yachting Magazine*. How she came to sink at such an appropriate moment no one seems to know. Perhaps someone gained by her sinking, certainly there was not much left of her to be lost. The worm must already at that time have begun to attack her—if not through her bottom where she would still have been protected by the careful coatings of tar and the antique anti-borer concoctions put on by Captain Culler, then where her stem was damaged and where bare timber was exposed to the warm and organic tropical water. If some foul play was responsible, no person was ever brought to book. The Receiver of Wrecks, in whose charge she was, had kept her pumped out and at least afloat for over three years since Geoffrey Innes had departed. She had been covered with at least some old tarpaulins and although she had deteriorated she was still recognisable as a yacht. Once on the bottom she became the property of the Crown and, to all intents and purposes, worthless. A derisory bid of $1 was received for her and she was withdrawn from the auction.

Not surprisingly, she was later sold, still on the bottom, for $100. I know very little of the $100 purchaser. I know he raised her from the bottom with the intention of having her towed to Miami—but he could find no takers for the towing job, at least within the price he had set as a realistic one. Then, as far as I know, he systematically stripped her of everything he could find of the slightest value. Anchors, chains, the alloy cylinder head of the main engine, pumps, auxiliaries, copper pipe, the fine panelling in the owner's cabin, lavatory fittings, bilge pumps, brass light fittings from the cabin—the lamps themselves had long since disappeared—cabin table, any likely timber that was portable, iron work from round the deck, all the electrical sockets and switches and much of the wiring itself and any movable pieces of rope or wire or stores of any kind that were left in her—everything was taken. Perhaps for his $100 he also got the *Integrity's* inlaid wheel which Geoffrey Innes, although he would dearly have liked to have kept it for himself, put in store for safety. It alone was worth four times what he paid for the yacht. After he had taken everything he could find of value, perfectly sensibly and justifiably it should be said, the $100 purchaser went on his way, leaving the *Integrity* once more unattended. In due course she sank again. She remained on the bottom for nearly two years. She was on the bottom when Bill moved into his boatyard, she was still there when Ron Bamber bought her. He paid $1,000 for her.

Why it took Ron Bamber so long to buy the *Integrity* I

find it hard to understand. Clearly he wanted her with more than ordinary determination. He had tried to buy her when she first came to Turks—surely he could have pursued his negotiations with Geoffrey Innes to a successful conclusion? He must have known that she had been bought for just a tenth of the sum he gave for her a matter of years previously, that she had been stripped bare of every movable solid object, or almost so, and that she must have deteriorated to the point of worthlessness in the interval. It is a mystery that puzzled me at the time and has puzzled me ever since. Because Bill was on the spot, Bamber employed him to raise the *Integrity*. Incredibly, it seemed later to me and then to everyone else, Bamber intended to make the *Integrity* seaworthy, or as seaworthy as could be, have her towed to Cat Island and there have her rebuilt. Cat Island is a fairly straightforward journey from Grand Turk, 300 miles to the north west up the Bahamas chain of islands. There should be no particular navigational dangers—the route is along the windward side of the islands and is all in deep water.

There is no slipway in Cat Island but I was told that some form of slip was to be constructed and the *Integrity* was to be dragged out of the water and up the beach by some undefined method—perhaps man-power, or a bulldozer or some kind of winch. Once hauled out, she was to be rebuilt, using labour that was already available in Cat Island. Whether or not the labour was really of the quality necessary to undertake such a task is doubtful. Skilled shipwrights would be needed with the right materials readily to hand—caulkers, blacksmiths, engineers, riggers—all far away from the resources of Cat Island. Even if there was no structural damage to her except the broken stem, the cost of making her again what she had once been would be astronomical. Waldo himself, with all the advantages of the Concordia Yard at his disposal, spent an enormous sum of money on her original building—it would have cost Ron Bamber many times more. It occurred to me, fancifully perhaps, that the *Integrity* may have contained some secret treasure or some asset of enormous value that was known to Ron Bamber and to no one else and that it was to gain some priceless advantage that he was anxious to throw his good money after her with such profligacy. Bill, with Chauncey to help him as and when possible, set about the task of raising the *Integrity*. As far as I could gather they got her up, or half up, and then some disagreement developed between Bill and Ron Bamber and she was allowed to sink to the bottom again. By this time, perhaps, she was growing weary of the wars that were being fought over her and would have been pleased enough to have been left in peace on the soft, pale yellow sand at the bottom of Hawk's Nest anchorage with the crystal Bahamian waters washing over her. It was not to be. Ron Bamber commissioned another group of salvors who did raise the *Integrity*. I do not know whether they were outsiders and I do not know how they did it. At all events when *Iskra* arrived in Hawk's Nest the *Integrity* was afloat, there was a motor pump on her deck which was run every four hours during the day. It discharged a gush of yellow water which tumbled across the deck, flooded the scuppers and poured itself back into the ocean.

As I sat at the end of Bill's jetty, dangling my legs idly and looking at the *Integrity* and *Iskra* beside her, I began to work out in my mind how *Iskra* could tow the *Integrity* for 300 miles and I began to wonder whether it was practicable. The more I thought about it and the more I looked at the two yachts the more surely I came to the conclusion that it was. *Iskra's* engine is not powerful but it is steady and reliable—an old Ailsa Craig diesel with a big, heavy flywheel. On the basis of its performance for the five years I have known *Iskra* there was no reason why it should not run at its steady even pace for as long as it was given fuel. Since I have known it nothing has ever soured the sweetness of its beat—nothing has ever gone wrong with it that could not be repaired by the exercise of common sense and with the use of a spanner, a piece of wire or, in extreme cases of recalcitrance, a tap with a hammer. It has about it a sort of timeless reliability which is almost boring. It uses no oil to speak of and it runs for two and a

107

half hours on one gallon of fuel. But I would use the sails to tow the *Integrity*. Towing is an art that requires patience—the slower you go the more likely you are to arrive. I reckoned that with the wind behind or on the quarter *Iskra* would tow the *Integrity* at between two and three knots. If sail could be set on the yacht's stump of a mast this might even be improved on. If the weather behaved as it has always behaved the wind should be from the east, the north-east or the south-east for most of the time. Even if it did swing into the north and blow for a spell, with plenty of sea room it would be possible to hold the *Integrity* clear of danger. I stood up on the end of the jetty and looked around. There was no one about, only Bill engaged in some task in the boatyard. I dropped into my rubber dinghy which was tied to the jetty, rowed out to the *Integrity* and climbed on board. I was in no way prepared for what I saw.

She was a ghost, hauled from the dead back into the harsh and brittle light. What she had to show would have been better left in the modest obscurity of the sea bed. She had the appearance and the stench of death about her—she was putrid and unclean. My instinct was to leave her at once and to forget the project—to go back to the wholesomeness of *Iskra* and to pursue my own business. In the misery of her ruin I was checked from flight only by that strange quality of worth and essential virtue which the schooner gave off. I believe that any sailor with the essence of the sea in his veins would have been arrested by the same quality. It is like the attraction between a man and a woman, incapable of analysis, defying rational understanding, which can draw two people together, or a person and a boat together, inexorably until they are fixed with iron bonds. She was rotten like cheese. Her decks were traced all over with the marks of worm. There was no vestige of paint left on her, her broken mast stuck up towards the sky like a decayed tooth, her smashed hatches and the broken taffrail made her look crooked and debauched. She was covered with a thin green slime so that it was difficult to stand on deck. Yet, out of her

108

humiliation another, undefinable quality was to be seen—she was from the aristocracy—there was no hiding it.

For a moment I hesitated and then I went below, through the broken companionway into the owner's cabin aft, treading gingerly down the smashed ladder. It was like climbing into the body of a huge, dead whale. A thick mist of tiny brown insects attacked me with voracious zeal—the stench of rot and decay was sickening—trailers of green weed hung from the deck and draped themselves over the bulk heads—everything I touched was covered in slime and seemed soft, as if it could be broken away with the hand. I believe the coral had begun to form round her contours, the tiny creatures at once consuming her and encrusting her in a mask of gaudy decoration. The floorboards were ripped up and some were missing, bulkheads were smashed, skin fittings and the twisted remains of plumbing where the lavatories had been wrenched out, made a grotesque tracery of broken pipes— the block of the six cylinder engine, covered in a green shroud was like the coffin of some departed freebooter laid to rest in a phantom tomb. For years she had been the home of bright tropical creatures who had peopled her with the gay colours and strange configurations of the mysterious world of under the sea. Shoals of scarlet, bright green and vivid blue had made her their familiar haunt, wandering through her ample caverns like groups of undersea tourists visiting some mausoleum, darting, turning, diving and climbing with the unison of their incomprehensible discipline. She had forgotten the glories and admirations of her past and had been re-incarnated into a new world of movement and colour—a world full of beauty and violence. Squid and octopus and the marauders of the deep had sought refuge in her, playing out the ever pressing tensions of their struggle to survive, sometimes motionless, tense and watchful, sometimes moving to kill with swift and savage thrusts of power. She had become no longer part of the world of light and air and soft cool breezes but a creature of dusky twilight, tuned for ever to her new element and content to be a part of it.

Everywhere there was the trickle and bubble and patter of dripping water. She had been pumped out not an hour before—I had seen the man come in a car, as I sat on Bill's jetty, go on board and run the motor pump for half an hour and then depart. Already the water was welling up over the floor. It was bubbling through the garboards, I could hear it running down inside the hull behind the wooden lining, could see it cascading through the stem like a miniature waterfall. She was all stuck together with some patent underwater cement. It had been plastered round the broken stem and poked between the dead wood and the planking so that she looked pock-marked with brown splodges. She had a feeling of eerie insecurity about her as though at any moment she might decide that enough was enough, spring apart at the seams and sink immediately to the bottom where she now belonged—taking with her any person who was unwise enough to be on board. I was over-taken by a sudden fear and at the same time a sudden resolution. I ran to the ladder and gained the deck, shaking the insects out of my nose and ears, taking deep draughts of the pure, crisp air of the morning. I tumbled over the side into my dinghy and rowed swiftly ashore. I ran up the jetty, causing it to swing and shake—into Bill's hut, through the end part where he lived with his bunk, his cooking stove, his table and seats made from driftwood, his books and his lamp hanging from a beam. Bill was sitting on a coil of rope mending a fishing net. "Hey Bill—for Christ's sake, why the hell don't we tow the bloody *Integrity* to Cat?" Bill looked up and slowly put to one side the net and the reel of twine and then he said in his low, slow drawl, "Why Jesus, man—why don't we do that?"

"Why Jesus, man — why don't we do that?"

MR INNES,
    MY QUESTION IS.
IF YOU RECIEVE
FUNDS FOR
SALVAGE — MAY
WE S~~TEADER~~ SHARE
IN THAT AMOUNT
?

THIS IS DANGEROUS
ENOUGH AT SEA
TO MERRIT A SHARE
NEVER... MIND
THE INCREDIBLE WORK

CHAPTER XI

Bill thought we ought to charge Bamber $1,500 for the tow. I found it hard to believe that anyone would be prepared to pay out that much good money for the *Integrity,* but I agreed. I believe Bill looked on me as something of a simpleton, which in some respects I suppose I am. He didn't think I was a match for Ron Bamber in a business deal. He cautioned me, "If you're in a business deal, no matter who it's with, you've got to watch it man." We decided that Bill was to be on board the *Integrity;* Paul, Heather's assistant in her tropical fish business whom I had met on my first night in Turks, would come with me in *Iskra.* We agreed to split everything we got from the job four ways—one share for each of us and one share for *Iskra,* the boat's share to pay the expenses. Allowing an average speed of two knots the voyage would take six days. We would have to spend at least a couple of days in preparation—there would be a lot to do. We talked about the job for the whole evening. Bill would have to live on deck—under some sort of tent or awning—no one could live below on the *Integrity,* she was too foul. Paul had never been sailing but he had been on ships and motorboats often enough and he swore to me that he had never in his life been sea-sick. That he had no experience didn't worry me—it might be a

113

positive advantage—it would make it easier for him to do what I wanted him to do without question. On the other hand, if he was prone to sea-sickness he would be a liability. Sea-sickness is a dangerous disease in small boats. It destroys a man's ability, it adds another worry and it undermines morale. Moreover, it occurs at the beginning of a voyage which is the most dangerous time for a single-handed or short-handed crew. In the first days the crew are not yet accustomed to sea routine—they are used to being asleep all night and awake all day. At sea, you must be awake equally by day and by night and you must sleep in short spells of no more than two hours spread through the day and night. It takes time to establish this routine—perhaps two or three days before the body is tuned to a state of constant alertness. In the first days a man gets overtired and then neither his brain nor his body are operating efficiently.

I discovered, by chance, from the Windjammer Hotel, where Ron Bamber was well known, that arrangements were already in hand to have the *Integrity* towed to Cat Island. In fact there was a high-powered American in the hotel who had come to Turks specifically to look at the yacht and to quote for the job. I saw him at the other end of the bar—a tall, quiet man with short cropped hair and light blue eyes. I understood he had a powerful diesel motor cruiser somewhere in the islands which was capable of towing the *Integrity* and that Bamber had asked him for a price. I was given this information by a young Scotsman I met in the bar who also told me that Bamber was coming to Turks in his private aeroplane the next afternoon, to confer with the American. Clearly, if I was to stand a chance of being considered, I would have to speak to Bamber before he concluded with the American. By asking discreetly, I found out that for some reason, Bamber could not be telephoned on Cat Island. I managed to get the address of his hotel before I left the Windjammer. I went a few doors along the straggle of houses and Government offices and stores to the Cable and Wireless establishment—a spacious bungalow with a flagpole in the front garden. I sent Ron Bamber a

114

cable with a message which I hoped would attract his interest without telling him too much. "Telephone me Cable and Wireless Turks tomorrow nine about *Integrity*." Then I went to Chauncey's house where I found Bill and Paul and Chauncey and Heather all sitting on the verandah. As I climbed the steps the sun was setting into the sea on the other side of South Caicos. I helped myself to a can of beer from the fridge and joined them. "Well—we've started," I said.

At nine the next morning I went to the Cable and Wireless office and sat on a chair in the waiting room. At eleven no phone call had come. I decided to wait until a quarter past eleven and then to abandon it. It was a long shot in any case. The chances were that Bamber would think *Iskra* not powerful enough for the job and settle with the American. At ten past eleven the Bahamian girl telephonist called through the hatch, the pride of achievement in her voice. "You Mulville sir? I got a call here man—all de way from Cat Island." I went into a small cubicle. "Hello—is that Mr. Bamber?" there was a loud, sustained crackle. "Is that Bamber? BAM-BER?" The crackle increased in intensity, swelling in volume like a train in a tunnel. Somewhere within it there was a voice—far, far away a faint and feeble echo of a voice so thin as to be hardly there. "What do you want?" "Tow *Integrity* to Cat— fifteen hundred dollars—one thousand five hundred dollars." Perversely, the crackle increased, swelling until the voice was the merest shadow within it. "See you tomorrow— Windjammer—three o'clock." I put the phone down, sweating. The telephonist opened her hatch. "That will be ten dollars." "But he called me—I didn't call him." "That's ten dollars", she said. "But I couldn't hear—bad line—all crackle." "That's just ten dollars." I gave her ten dollars with a twinge of pain— I could live for at least three days on ten dollars. My voyage was on a shoe-string—it was being paid for by magazine articles I sent back to England every two weeks and I was parsimonious to the point of eccentricity. I didn't mind spending money on fun but a telephone call—particularly an inaudible one was a different matter. I was beginning to get

115

tired of the *Integrity*—Bill and I and Chauncey and Paul had been talking about nothing else for the past two days. Now, apart from wasting my time she was beginning to cost me money. Time was against me too. I had promised to be in Nassau for Tamarind's birthday—I would almost certainly be late. I walked back to *Iskra* along the road over the salt pans, past the NASA base where the enormous aerial swept the boundless blue sky with its invisible, electronic proboscis. It was a satellite tracking station—a key link in a chain of similar contrivances which encircle the earth rather as the standing stones and monoliths of pre-history. Perhaps they serve a similar, esoteric purpose. I went on board and mended *Iskra's* bobstay.

The next morning Bill brought me from Hawk's Nest on the back of the motor cycle. Through the roar of the exhaust he turned half round and yelled into my ear, "Ask him for a half in advance—he'll beat you down—don't accept less than a third." Everyone in Turks knew it when Bill was abroad on his motor cycle—it made more noise than Ron Bamber's aeroplane. As we roared past the Windjammer we saw heads peer down from the bougainvillea-covered verandah—the tall American and the Scotsman. The word must have got around that I was interested in the *Integrity*. We stopped outside Chauncey's house, climbed the steps to the verandah, reaching into the fridge for a beer as we passed. Chauncey and Heather were not at home. We sat in wicker chairs balancing our feet on the verandah rail and yet again rehearsed over in our minds what gear we would need and how the job was to be done. Bill never doubted that Bamber would accept our offer although we had no knowledge of what terms the tall American had put forward. I didn't believe that the American or the Scotsman had any inkling that we were going to offer to tow the *Integrity*. It would never have occurred to them that such a job could be done under sail and they would conclude that *Iskra's* engine was far and away too small and weak for such a task. I was sure that Ron Bamber, when he saw *Iskra*, would reject the notion

116

that she could tow *Integrity*. I thought that in common with most people, he would never believe that a long tow could be done under sail with the aid of a comparatively small engine, in spite of the fact that the old *Captain Cap,* with her cut down rig, had brought the *Integrity* in to Turks under sail. I was wrong. One man apart from Bill and me did believe it— Ron Bamber.

Bill saw the aeroplane first—a speck the size of a trouser button growing quickly out of the dazzling blue and the white clouds scattered like random pieces of a child's jigsaw. It banked low overhead and as it whistled softly past we could see Bamber sitting at the controls, inclining his head and gazing down on us. "Time you stroll down to the Windjammer", Bill said, "he'll be there. Remember—he's tough—watch it." I walked along the sandy road and climbed to the first floor of the hotel. The tall American and the Scotsman were there with another man—a native of Turks. I nodded to him—I had seen him that morning—it was he who came to Hawk's Nest every four hours to run the *Integrity's* pump. The Scotsman asked me, "Did you speak to Ron Bamber?" I mumbled something about a bad line and he said, "Are you interested in the *Integrity*?" I answered him evasively, "Well. . . I might be." They moved away from the bar and we all of us waited patiently and separately for Bamber to arrive, not exchanging a further word or a glance. He soon came bustling in with an air of nervous vitality. "You Mulville?" he said, curtly. "Yes." "See you in my room—number 4, downstairs. Go down and wait for me." Then he went across to the other group. He was a small man, balding with bright, quick grey eyes. He seemed to move in jerks like a clockwork toy. He wore a light, tropical suit, immaculately pressed with a blue silk handkerchief just showing from the top pocket and a ring with a yellow stone on the right index finger. The little flashing eyes were cold and impersonal, gathering information from every quarter— storing it away in a small computer which must have been ticking away somewhere inside where other people keep a heart. "I'll be down in ten minutes."

The room was a small single. Bamber's grip, unopened, was on the bed. I sat on an upright chair and waited for exactly ten minutes and then he came in, proffered me his hand and sat down on the edge of the bed. The eyes took in every aspect of my being with sudden, rapid blinks I felt as if they were feeling round inside my mind, extracting, logging, appraising and filing away in the computer for future use. "What's your proposition?" he said. I told him I was in Turks only by chance—that I had seen the *Integrity*, had heard that he required her to be towed to Cat Island, that I had been on board her, had studied the problem as a seaman and as one experienced in ocean towing and that I was confident that, if he wanted me to quote, I could do the job with my boat. "What's your price?" he said. "Fifteen hundred dollars—one half payable at once and the balance on arrival with the tow in Cat Island." The grey eyes blinked nervously and narrowed for an instant. The computer was at work. "I accept your price but not your terms. I'll pay you one third now—cash tomorrow morning—and the balance on arrival—agreed?" I shrugged—it was no less than Bill had advocated. "Agreed," I said. "Come back in an hour's time and I'll confirm it." He got up and opened the door for me. I went along a passage and out into the sudden sunlight. Bamber watched me go and then walked briskly back up the stairs to make his peace with the tall American and the Scotsman—to compensate them for their wasted time or at least to refund them their expenses for their journey to Turks. I walked back again from the Windjammer to Chauncey's house. Chauncey and Heather and Paul and Bill were all on the verandah and I felt their eyes on me as I walked towards the house. But these were relaxed, friendly eyes—eyes full of sympathy, help and encouragement. "We're in business," I said, "Bamber will give us five hundred dollars tomorrow morning and we start."

As I was going back to the Windjammer an hour later Bamber arrived at Chauncey's house. He was driving a battered old hired car which I knew belonged to the man who did the pumping—he had asked me, when he saw *Iskra* in Hawk's Nest, whether I wanted to hire it. Bamber said, "Okay, it's confirmed. I want you to draw up an agreement between us—two copies. We'll sign it tomorrow morning when I give you the money." Then he said, "Come and have dinner with me tonight—at eight o'clock", and finally, before he let in the clutch, "You're responsible for running the pump—as from now. There's no gas on board." I said, "I'll look after the pump but not from now—from tomorrow morning." I watched the computer digest. The grey eyes were frozen—they were not eyes that liked to be crossed. "Okay—from tomorrow morning", and he was gone. Chauncey said to me, on the verandah, "You're taking a big risk Frank—suppose the *Integrity* sinks somewhere along the line—maybe half way between here and Cat—with all your stores and gear on board. Suppose the pump goes wrong and you can't keep her afloat or suppose she just breaks up. You'll have to ship the boys back to Turks by air. You'll lose on the deal."

I hoped there would be the chance to put this point to Ron Bamber at dinner but it was a large party and I didn't like to raise it. I thought it odd that he had asked me to formulate the agreement instead of doing it himself—perhaps he really trusted me, perhaps I had gained the opposite impression through a misinterpretation of his manner. I didn't like the emphasis on written agreements, I would have gone into the business on the basis of mutual trust—a method I have used over and over again and have almost always found satisfactory. If you trust a man and he trusts you the bond is far stronger than any written agreement. It is easy to pick holes in an agreement and to bend the words to your own ends—the mere fact of having such a document encourages you to do so. But an understanding over a handshake is unbreakable. It allows for compromise and accommodation and when the affair is finished with, both sides find themselves anxious that the other should have had a fair deal. This makes business into a pleasure. Perhaps a lifetime of cut and thrust in the American business jungle had left its mark on Ron
119

Bamber. I wasn't interested in this affair only for money, any more than Geoffrey Innes had been when he towed the *Integrity* to Turks. On the other hand if there was money to be made, I would be the last to turn away my face.

The tall American and the Scotsman were at dinner—they were obviously upset and said very little. By keeping the conversation general—boats, politics, the weather, women, we got through the evening without mishap. Afterwards Bamber drove me back to Hawk's Nest. I told him that Bill and Paul would be my crew and he made no comment. I asked him if he would fly them back from Cat Island to Turks when the tow was completed but he refused. He said it was very difficult for him to do this and it would have to be my responsibility. The next morning I was up early. I looked across at the *Integrity*'s bedraggled form as it took substance from the dawn and realised that as from now, she was my responsibility. I rowed across to her with a can of petrol I had brought from the town, filled the tank on the motor pump, wound on the starting cord and pulled. The pump fired, coughed and then ran. The gush of brown water swilled round my bare feet on the deck. I went below and stepped into a foot of water at the bottom of the ladder. The insects, delighted to find themselves visited so early in the morning, sank their sharp teeth into my face, neck, arms and legs. As I retreated up the ladder my foot slipped off the bottom rung. To save myself from falling I clutched at the edge of a shallow wooden shelf which ran across the after part of the owner's cabin. My hand came against something of metal— something hard and solid. When I regained my balance I took the object off the shelf and carried it out on deck. It was the bronze boss from the *Integrity*'s wheel—a simple thing but it had about it the quality of excellence which I could not help associating with the *Integrity*. As I looked at it in my hand it made her present plight seem all the sadder. The pump ran for nearly an hour before the *Integrity* was dry. I stopped it and went back to *Iskra*. I dropped the boss into my bo'sun's box where a hundred worthy things are kept—palm and needle, beeswax, twine, scissors, spike and fid—one day it might come in for something. I left it there and forgot all about it.

It took me an hour, sitting at *Iskra's* cabin table and sweating over my portable typewriter to formulate Bamber's agreement. In the end it was a simple document, I have no doubt riddled with legal anomalies, in which I undertook to tow the *Integrity* and Bamber undertook to pay the money. At the end I put in an extra clause, "Mr. Bamber shall purchase two airline tickets for the crew to return to Grand Turk Island before the operation begins." Then Bill took me to town on the motor cycle, dropping me off at the Windjammer. Bamber sat on his bed and read the agreement. When his eyes reached the last paragraph I saw them consume it with rapacious blinks, saw the computer grind out its predictable reaction. "I can't accept that", he said, jabbing his finger with the ring against the offending words. "You said $1,500— now you're asking for more." I explained the difficulty— explained how I might easily be let in for a substantial loss. "If we make it to Cat Island," I said, "you can have the tickets back and the boys will pay their own fares—or I'll pay them—there will be no problem. Or, if you like, you can undertake to fly them back yourself. I don't want to make extra money out of the fares," I explained to him, "I just want to cover myself in case the job goes wrong." He wouldn't accept it. "You said $1,500," he repeated, "now you want more." I thought the whole thing was off and really, I wasn't sorry. I got up to go. I said, "Don't worry about it Mr. Bamber. To be honest, I don't really mind whether I do the job or not. Your American friend is still here—you can conclude with him as if I had never been in the deal." My hand was on the door handle when he said, "Wait a minute. I'll pay half the fares—I'll give you the cash now." I thought for a moment—it was a compromise and it would be churlish to reject it, although I didn't like it and I didn't like the way it was done. I said, "Alright—I accept."

Ron Bamber went to see the bank, drew out the money

121

and gave it to me—five hundred and seventy dollars. Then we both went to Chauncey's house where we found Bill. Bamber wanted Bill to salvage the *Integrity's* windlass which for some reason was on the bottom at Hawk's Nest. He wanted it put on board and taken to Cat. There were various things belonging to him that were in Bill's boatyard and we all went there together to decide what gear was to go with the *Integrity*. There was a spare pump to be put on board in case of a breakdown and an inflatable raft—a large, round affair, surplus U.S. government equipment. It would be useful and it would serve as a life raft for Bill. Bamber didn't wish to go on board the *Integrity* or on board *Iskra* although I offered to take him. In fact he hardly looked at *Iskra* and he didn't ask any questions about my plans for the tow. He wanted me to call in at one of the islands on the way to Cat although for obvious reasons of navigation it was out of the question to take the *Integrity* into a reef-strewn and dangerous anchorage at Providenciales Island. As far as he was concerned, towing was something you paid money for which was, I suppose, a reasonable attitude. He didn't pretend to know anything about seamanship any more than I could understand the obscure and devious paths of business. He may have thought that having agreed to do the job and having accepted his payment it was ungracious of me to refuse what he thought of as a simple request. I never understood for certain why he wanted me to call at Providenciales. I believe that the American's motor boat was there. I don't believe he had any conception of what was really involved in what he was trying to do with the *Integrity*. He had seen pictures of her in yachting magazines and had convinced himself that she was his ideal.

Bill and Paul and I took him to the airfield from the Hawk's Nest. He had two passengers—the Scotsman and the American. As we all stood on the tarmac I tried to reach some point of contact and understanding with the American. "I'm sorry," I said to him, "I didn't want to do you out of this job if you really need it." The American looked straight at me and I saw his face suddenly relax. The haughty look which he normally wore was driven away by a kind, sympathetic smile. "Have a good trip," he said. "I hope it all goes well. Good luck," and he shook me by the hand. We watched them climb into the aeroplane and we watched it sail away across the sky. I took the roll of bank notes from my pocket and gave $125 to Bill and the same to Paul. Then I said, "Right—we're in business. Now we must get moving—we've a lot to do."

It was the bronze boss from the Integrity's wheel.

CHAPTER XII

Bill said he would live on peanut butter—it was the elixir of life to him—he needed nothing else. I gave Heather a list of stores and she undertook to get them for us from the PX— the store in the American base. *Iskra* was already well provided with stores for Paul and me. We ordered more and Bill found a load of tins stacked under a heap of decaying rope and canvas in the yard which he gave us. Petrol for the pump was a problem. It was cheap but there was a chronic shortage of drums on the island. In the end, Chauncey found us an old 50-gallon drum somewhere round the back of his house— enough petrol to keep the pump running for one third of the time, which was twice as much time as it was run at anchor in the Hawk's Nest. We tested the drum, cleaned it out and decided that it would serve. I would need extra diesel for *Iskra* and we scoured the island for drums but could find none. We used kerosene tins and two of Bamber's water cans which had been put on board for shipment to Cat. This gave us enough diesel for 150 hours under engine—given a reasonable wind it would be sufficient.

Bamber had been astonishingly concerned about any odd pieces of gear that belonged to the *Integrity* or to him. Before he went he looked over Bill's yard like a gold prospector searching for anything that was his. He had made a pile of what seemed to Bill and me the most outrageous junk which he insisted should be put on board the *Integrity*. I don't believe he was so much concerned for the things for their own sake as he was that he should take everything that belonged to him, regardless of its worth. I sympathised with him— he had got very little of value for his $1,000 let alone the money he had spent and was spending on the *Integrity*. I had made it perfectly clear to him that my own concern was in towing the *Integrity* and that her condition and seaworthiness was no affair of mine. He had told us that she had already been prepared for towing and that nothing remained to be done before we set off. All that was necessary was to run the pump for half an hour every four hours and everything would be alright. When Bill and I went on board and looked at her with dispassionate eyes, we saw that there was much to be done.

Bill and Paul and I worked as hard as we could on the *Integrity* and on *Iskra* for three days. Bill found several old tea chests in his yard—put by at some time in case they should come in useful—which we used for covering the hatches and broken skylights. We cut tingles and hammered them on over every opening in the deck except the hatch in the owner's cabin which Bill would use. He would not sleep in the owner's cabin but would use it to store his food and cooking gear. We used six-inch nails to spike the tingles over the openings—it was difficult to find hard wood to hammer into. We would strike the nails—the first blow would pierce the tea chest and the second would sink the nail to its head. We through-fastened the two pumps to the cabin top by banging nails through the deck and turning them over—the only way to make them secure. We made two houses for the pumps— a wooden framework covered with the invaluable tea chests and strips of old canvas. If the weather was bad she would ship water all over the deck and unless the pumps were protected they would never run. We made a cradle for the petrol drum so that it could be tilted by a man alone and a

126

small can filled from it. We rigged a framework from the mast stump aft to spread one of *Iskra's* old sails and we contrived fastenings for Bill's hammock. When he had finished it looked cosy. Bill would be able to take his ease in the shade or the sun depending on his whim—lying on the deck like a film star, watching the flying fish, savouring the sea breezes, slaking his appetite with peanut butter—and being paid for it. Paul said, "You'll like it here. Man—when we get to Cat you won't want to come ashore." I fastened a stout life-line from for'ard to aft along the deck—we fitted preventer lines to the stump of the tiller.

There was nothing at all left of Captain Culler's steering gear which had been copied from Slocum's *Spray*. The stub-end of the tiller running aft from the top of the rudder post with its elaborate system of ropes and pulleys and blocks to the wheel, had all either been pillaged, broken or had rotted away. Now there was a longer tiller—or to be more accurate a piece of unfinished soft wood nailed to the head of the rudder post—which faced for'ard. We had no intention of steering the *Integrity,* she would find her own course behind *Iskra* depending on wind and weather, but we might easily wish to give her a bias one way or the other. Accordingly we rigged lines to the bulwarks from the end of the crude stump so that Bill could adjust the yacht's sheer. I had no idea what sort of shape the rudder pintles were in. Certainly the way the tiller was fastened to the rudder was crude in the extreme. The latest work on the *Integrity* had evidently been done in a makeshift fashion as if by someone who did not believe she was any longer worth taking trouble over. Bill and I did our best to redeem a poorly cobbled job but neither of us were carpenters and in any case, the work was strictly outside the limits of our contract.

Heather provided for us from the PX a huge aerosol canister, a thing the size of a cannon barrel, filled with some deadly poison which would kill everything that moved. It was like a death ray gun in a child's comic. Bill sprayed round the inside of the hull, a wet handkerchief tied round his face, and the insects fell in their hordes. Nothing could take the stench of decay away from her but at least now it was possible to go below without being eaten. I put *Iskra's* spare primus cooking stove on board, which sits in a home-made gimbal of its own, with a supply of methylated spirit, paraffin and prickers. In spite of Bill's avowed intention to live on peanut butter, I gave him a selection of tins and packets to last him for eight days, a saucepan and *Iskra's* spare kettle. "Look after the kettle", I said to him, "it's a friend." It had been with me on many voyages—with it's snub nose and its zany whistle, it had forged for itself a place in my affections. We scrubbed out what had been the owner's bunk with disinfectant and made a stores locker out of it. I provided him with a five gallon plastic can for his drinking water, a tin opener, a knife, a spoon and a fork, there was a Tilley lamp on board which belonged to Bamber, a torch, spare batteries and a copy of *Pilgrim's Progress.* "Keep your mind occupied and free from base thoughts." While Bill was spraying round in the engine room, as had happened to me the previous day, his hand came in contact with something solid. He pulled out from behind the engine a strip of heavy gauge brass, four or five inches wide and four feet long, which he brought on deck and gave to me. "Better keep this safe," he said; "it's worth more than the boat." I took it on board and stowed it in the fo'c'sle. We agreed it would be better in *Iskra's* fo'c'sle until we got to Cat when we would present it to Bamber.

On board *Iskra* I allowed Paul a shelf for his few belongings and he settled himself in, pleased enough with his surroundings. He knew how to cook, he was tidy and he was easy to get on with. It would be pleasant to have somebody with me—I could not have towed the *Integrity* by myself. The most pressing task was to rig a towing bridle that would allow *Iskra* to be steered while she was towing—a job that needed some thought. A yacht, particularly a cutter like *Iskra,* makes a poor tug. This is because the tow line has to be fastened right aft in order to be clear of such things as the main sheet, the boom gallows and, in *Iskra,* the self steering gear. With a heavy weight fastened to her stern no yacht will steer. I believe the *Captain Cap* was able to tow the *Integrity* because she was much bigger and therefore had enough weight and power to pull herself round when she wished to turn, dragging the *Integrity* with her. *Iskra,* being smaller and lighter, would not be able to do this, she would be at the mercy of the wind and would go where it dictated—which might not be to Cat Island. A real tug, of course, tows from a hook which is amidships, in the centre of the tug's turning radius.

To overcome this difficulty I devised my own steering system. I made a bridle with two legs about thirty feet long spliced into a heavy bow shackle to which the main tow line would be attached. The in-board ends of the bridle dropped over *Iskra's* samson posts, one on either side of the after deck, offering a clear run aft. I had on board a tackle with two single blocks—a gun tackle to use the proper term—each block having a hook. One end of the tackle was hooked to the chain plates amidships, to a strop made specially for the purpose and the other to one leg of the bridle. By heaving short, I could transfer the weight of the tow from aft to amidships, on either side and so be able to turn either way. By changing the tackle from one side to the other *Iskra* could be put about and settled on another course. Once settled, both ends of the bridle were dropped onto their respective samson posts. The arrangement was a simple one in practice. It worked perfectly although it almost involved us in disaster.

As it happened, I had on board *Iskra* a long, heavy piece of very strong plastic line which made an ideal tow rope. It was long enough and heavy enough for the bight always to hang in the water. Even under maximum strain it never lifted clear of the sea and therefore it always had give in it and would never jerk. I believe I must have put it on board with such a job as towing in my mind.

Although Bill had his basic stores on board *Integrity* it was never my intention that he should stay there without a break for the whole passage. If the weather was reasonable he

129

would occasionally be able to transfer himself to *Iskra* in the float, when the pump was not running. We rigged a strong painter to the float with a shackle which he could fasten to the tow line. *Iskra* would heave-to or slow down and Bill would haul himself aboard with the shackle sliding along the rope as a preventer. We devised a system of signals and lights for basic communication and I gave him white flares for an emergency. Then Chauncey produced the ultimate amenity— a small, battery operated walkie-talkie. I never had much faith in the walkie-talkie. Bill's drawl wasn't easy to follow at any time but through these machines it was impossible. Paul swore he could understand every word. We were in a hurry to get everything ready and be off. We wanted to get the job done as quickly as possible because every day's delay was costing money. Everything takes a long time in Turks—life has a leisurely beat which cannot be hurried, there is always time. Bill and Paul dived for the *Integrity's* windlass, hauled it over the bow and got it down on the foredeck. I borrowed Heather's car and picked up the stores—I spent a day clearing customs, shuffling from one office to another, filling in forms, signing declarations. I found it almost impossible to communicate any sense of urgency to the man in the fuel office. At the last minute he announced that the fuel could not be delivered to Hawk's Nest because the truck driver was ill. It cost a day's patient persuasion to coax another driver to the job. We decided to employ the port pilot to take the *Integrity* out through the reef. Chauncey and Bill both knew the channel but it is a difficult passage and we thought it wise to take no chances. Chauncey was to tow the *Integrity* out using a powerful old boat that Bill had in the yard—an ex-government landing craft. Once clear of the reef Paul and I would connect *Iskra* and the tow proper would start.

The end of preparations came at last—everything was done that could be done. We had used all our resources and the thing was set up. On that last night I sat in *Iskra's* cockpit gazing across at the *Integrity* and applied every modicum of forethought that was in me, mobilised all the experience that could be brought to our aid. The night was without the moon, which was a pity for our purpose, but every star blazed with a special intensity as if to atone. Bill and Paul had gone off on the motor cycle. The immense roar of the machine grew fainter in ever diminishing waves of sound. I had come to know the road through the salt pans so perfectly that I could pinpoint their position by Bill's changes of gear and the machine's undulations as it curved and twisted on its way. The night was motionless, as if fixed in a block of glass. It had a tenseness, a brittle stillness too intense to be sustained, that must soon shatter into some furious activity. The *Integrity* was a black, mysterious outline drawn against the black waters of the Hawk's Nest anchorage. I wondered again at her power, was again astonished at her charisma. She had drawn me into her orbit along with a motley and disparate company—as I looked back on my association with her I began to understand the inevitability of it. That first moment when Bill had talked to me about her in his soft, musical voice, had led directly and inexorably to the present confrontation as we sized one another up across the lifeless black water. I felt again that she reproached me for my interference in her affairs—that she deeply resented the efficient and business-like preparations we had made for her removal from this place that she had come to regard as her last home—that our attentions were an inadmissible affront to her wishes. I wondered whether she could possibly survive this last traumatic reckoning—the odds were heavily stacked against her. It was my business to see that she did survive it. I would do my best but I sensed that I was acting against her wishes and desires—that she would fight me for the right to choose her own destiny.

I rowed ashore across the enamelled surface of the Hawk's Nest, climbed Bill's jetty and looked round at the ghostly and tumble down scattering of shacks which Bill called home. I felt a tinge of sadness for him in his loneliness. Bill was a loner and he paid a heavy price for his obsession. Heather's old car, also hired from the pumping man, took me swiftly to the comparative gaiety of the town. In the Windjammer couples

131

were dancing under the fragrance of the bougainvillea. Chauncey's house was a blaze of light. Everyone was there— a dinner party had been prepared. Heather had thrown open the gates of her generous and hospitable heart—there was laughter and conviviality, good humour, food, drink, optimism and the ring of cheerfulness. The sounds of our merriment floated free and unimpeded out across Chauncey's verandah, through the gently murmuring palms and away into the boundless and star-decked night towards Cat Island 300 miles to the west. For all that it was an auspicious and a confident sound I remember that even at that hour, standing apart and looking out from deep shadow across the ocean to the west, my thoughts went back to the subject of our optimism, riding to her scope sullen and unsmiling, with a death-wish in her heart.

The Integrity was a black mysterious outline drawn against the black waters of the Hawk's Nest anchorage.

CHAPTER XIII

The fine night continued itself into the following day. The sun came up, round and true and bright, mounting rapidly into a clear sky as if in a hurry to get the day properly started, impatient for everyone to be alert and about their business. Soon the trade wind clouds took up station round the horizon's rim making a frieze of formal decoration like the crocheted edge of a Victorian tablecloth. The breeze that sprang up from the east, gaining in strength as the day matured, confirmed the benign and settled state of the weather. I sniffed the dawn with approval and rowed over to the *Integrity*. I had left her for six hours instead of the regulation four hours, seduced by the gay conviviality of the previous evening. The pump ran for the best part of an hour. When I went on board she was visibly low in the water and inside, the locker seats in the fore cabin were already covered and the water was up to the tins in Bill's store and to the legs of the primus gimbal. The pump was efficient and easy to start. After it had been at work for half an hour I stopped it, transferred the hoses to the spare pump and ran that—to make quite certain that both pumps were operating properly. I had laid in spare sparking plugs, spare points and spare gaskets for the hoses. If the pumps broke down the *Integrity* would sink

133

without question. There was no possibility of keeping the water down by hand.

Bill was already up and about, I saw lights shining through the dawn with the incandescent brilliance induced by the crystal purity of the early morning atmosphere. I guessed he was making last minute additions and adjustments to his small mound—Bill was a man whose requirements were small and whose demands on this life were few.

We had breakfast together in *Iskra's* cabin, discussing the job for the hundredth time. Neither of us could think of any way in which we could improve on our preparations. Soon we heard the uneven noise of Heather's car as it advanced across the salt pans and saw over the flat, bleak terrain a steadily increasing puff of dust. She arrived with Chauncey and Paul, her eldest son Stewart and Sam the pilot. Chauncey and Bill started the engine of the landing craft and she was put alongside the *Integrity* and a tow line made fast. Then we all moved on board *Integrity* and sweated at her anchor. Under our combined attack it shifted out of the sand bottom where it had become deeply embedded, leaving the yacht fast by a second line attached to some immensely heavy piece of mooring equipment whose origins were known only to Bill. Paul and I went back to *Iskra,* leaving Bill in sole command of his charge. *Iskra's* second anchor was taken up and stowed and the chain shortened on her bower. The landing craft with Chauncey and Heather and Stewart and the pilot, streamed out the scope of the tow line and lay impatiently coughing and spluttering black smoke, waiting for the signal. Then Bill threw overboard the *Integrity's* mooring buoy and shouted, "Okay boys—let's go—it's shit or bust—next stop Cat Island." The landing craft's engine roared, the water churned from her stern, the tow line tightened and the *Integrity* began to move forward slowly and reluctantly. *Iskra's* anchor was brought on deck and we took station close astern, the old Ailsa Craig engine turning itself over with a leisurely, easy beat. There was no one to wave goodbye or to wish prosperity to our enterprise—only an old and mangy bird stood on one leg in the

134

shallows of the Hawk's Nest watching our departure with studied indifference.

Only an old and mangy bird stood on one leg in the shallows of Hawk's Nest, watching our departure with studied indifference.

The landing craft's diesel clattered lustily, the sound was thrown from rock to rock around the Hawk's Nest anchorage as the little convoy wound its way towards the ocean. It seemed that none of Bill's various modes of transport were strong in their exhaust systems. Bill steered the *Integrity* to keep her immediately astern of the landing craft, the roar of the reef grew steadily louder and clearer—soon we could see the breakers on our starboard hand, a long line of seething white—occasionally agitated through some flaw or secret orifice in the coral so that a great column would leap towards the sky, hover for an instant like a white ghost and then burst into a million particles to float gently back to its own element. The pilot gave a wave as we approached the gap and swung to starboard. The *Integrity* dipped and rose as she felt the ocean's swell under her keel once more, the colour of the sea changed again through the bands of its spectrum from palest green to

135

the robust blue of deep water, the reef passed astern with its rumble and we were away and free from the confines of the shore—into the limitless world of the open ocean.

Chauncey towed the *Integrity* for about a mile—until we had a good offing, well clear of the land abreast of the town and pointing north up the Turks Islands Passage. Paul and I already had the tow line fast to its bridle and flaked up and down *Iskra's* side deck on the port side. As I brought *Iskra* alongside the *Integrity's* starboard bow Bill let go the landing craft, took the end of the line from Paul and made it fast to another towing bridle we had already rigged on the *Integrity's* bow—a system of ropes led over the broken stem in such a way that they could not chafe and made fast round the stump of the foremast. The *Integrity* was rolling with a long, easy motion. The pump was running—the brown water swished from side to side across the deck and tumbled overboard through the scuppers. "How is she?" I asked Bill as *Iskra* came close. "Seems okay. She may be making a bit more—I'm not sure." It was calm in the Turks Islands Passage, still in the lee of the island—a perfect tropical morning. The wind freshened to Force 3 or 4, the sun shone with kindly tolerance, all was peaceful, hopeful and well disposed. "Nothing wrong with the weather," I said as I put *Iskra's* engine slow ahead and Paul began to pay out the tow line. "Not yet," Bill replied with the note of cynicism that was often in his voice. "This lady won't like it rough—no way." We waved him goodbye as we streamed the tow, taking care that the rope ran evenly over the side without a kink or snarl. When *Iskra* had taken it out to the bridle Paul threw the heavy shackle clear, I increased the engine speed and *Iskra* took the strain on the samson posts.

At first she didn't move. The strain came on the rope—I looked over the side—I glanced across at Chauncey standing-by a few yards off in the landing craft—Paul was steering, intent on the compass. Inside myself I was in panic. The *Integrity* was too heavy—*Iskra,* with her tiny engine would never do it. The whole thing was a giant miscalculation. I had made a monumental fool of myself—taken money under a huge false pretence—involved my friends in a situation of ridicule and contempt. I looked across at the *Integrity's* hulk rolling like a cow in the ocean's swell, a thin plume of blue smoke from the pump streaming off to leeward and the water pouring off her decks. Christ—that bloody American would get a good laugh out of this. And Bamber. He'd go mad. I'd have to repay him his down payment. Jesus—what a mess. I suppose I stood on *Iskra's* deck, leaning across the furled mainsail, full of despair, watching the motionless sea for nearly ten minutes of agony and humiliation before I noticed that she was moving. I remember when I was first at sea, standing on the dock in Buenos Aires and leaning my weight against the ship's iron plates. It took time but it could be done. My weight alone, in the end pushed the ship out until her ropes tightened. So it was with the *Integrity*. In five minutes she began imperceptibly to move—in a quarter of an hour she had steerage way and in half an hour she was ploughing across the ocean at all of two knots. I looked across at Chauncey again. His thumbs were turned up.

She was steering beautifully and the *Integrity* was in perfect station right astern. I went below and laid off a northerly course, to get us away from the land in the shortest possible time. I wouldn't be happy until we had an offing of at least twenty miles—then if it did blow a norther, I was confident that I could hold the *Integrity* clear of danger until it passed. Chauncey and Heather circled round us once with the landing craft and then they wished us good luck, everybody waved and they were gone, belching noise and black smoke into the clear morning air and consuming diesel at the rate of ten gallons an hour. The weather looked nothing if not propitious. The forecast from the meteorological station in Nassau, such as it was, gave a favourable prediction. I went on deck and hoisted the mainsail and the staysail, broke out the roller jib. The wind was from the east—on our starboard beam. It had eased a little but there was still enough for the sails to make a substantial addition to our speed. *Iskra*

137

heeled gently and as she felt the new power of her sails her speed increased to three knots—or perhaps a fraction more. It was midday. By nightfall we should have an offing and be able to square away on our course for Cat. I eased the engine revs to conserve fuel. We could do with a little bit more wind—up to Force 5 would suit us fine. Already Bill had set sail on the *Integrity's* stump and this too was making a difference. Paul had been steering with intense concentration, his eyes glued to the compass, not allowing his attention to wander for a moment. I relieved him and sent him below to make lunch for us.

Iskra was steering well. She lacked her usual responsiveness to the helm but it was not difficult to keep her on course. So far we had not used the adjustments on the bridle but if the wind freshened, I was sure that we would have to use the tackle. It was ready on the cabin top and it could be hooked to either leg of the bridle in seconds. Without the usual rush of water past the rudder she needed more weather helm. If the wind freshened much more we would have to put the tackle on the lee side to stop her from sheering into the wind. I wasn't sure how she would go when we turned on course for Cat Island and brought the wind aft. Unless she was going faster by then, which was possible, it would probably be necessary to take the mainsail down and set twin staysails to balance her. Down wind, if the trade blew as it knows how to blow, we would make four knots at least. Much depended on the weather. If it was fair and if the *Integrity* could be kept afloat, all would be well but these were two large and precarious questions.

After lunch we saw Bill waving from the bows of the *Integrity* and Paul talked to him on the radio. Everything was going well but the *Integrity* was leaking more. Bill said that every time she dipped on a swell the sea spurted in through the damaged stem. Some of the patent cement had come out. He wasn't sure whether the hood-ends had not begun to spring away from the rabbet in the stem. Bamber had left at least two drums of the cement on board. I told Bill to stuff some more

138

in—as much as he could. I had left him a trowel from *Iskra's* tool box, thinking that something like this might happen. Paul and I could tell that the *Integrity* was leaking more because now we could hear the pump more often and for longer spells. As we got clear of the land and met the ocean, the swell increased. We were doing well. Already Turks was no more than a thin line of sand faintly pencilled along the horizon to the south. By the time darkness came we would have the offing we needed and would be able to turn so that the swell and what sea there was would be behind us. Then, I hoped, the *Integrity* would leak less. I know I am an optimist. The vice has often led me into scrapes and jams that no sane man would ever become involved in. There is nothing I can do about it—I just believe, deep down inside, that in the end, whatever the risk everything will be all right. In the end everything usually is and so the vice feeds on itself and my optimism escalates until, inevitably, there is a crash. Strangely, when the rubble and dust has subsided, I find that everything is still more or less right.

We towed all afternoon maintaining our northerly course. There is a strange fascination about towing which I have often experienced but have never fully understood. When I was in the tug *Integrity* we towed a floating dock which had been used to lift the British battle fleet during the war across the Atlantic from Alexandria to Bermuda at roughly the same speed as *Iskra* was now towing the yacht *Integrity*. Earlier we had taken part in a much longer tow—the floating dock A.F.D. 17 from Reykjavik Fiord, Iceland, to Sydney, Australia in 1945—which must be the longest tow on record because Reykjavik and Sydney are two places as far apart in this world as it is possible to be. The bureaucrat in the Admiralty, either naval or civilian, who ordered this tow intended that A.F.D. 17 should be taken to Manus in the Pacific but by the time the dock reached Sydney, after nine months on passage, it was apparent even to the British Navy that A.F.D. 17 was a write-off. During the thirty-three days of the tow across the Indian Ocean between Cochin and

139

Freemantle and again the twenty days between Freemantle and Sydney, the long swells of the ocean had punched a hole twenty feet across in the bottom of the dock. The iron plates had opened upwards like the petals of some gigantic tropical flower. Every time the dock rose and fell the sea was forced up through the hole under enormous pressure, sending a column of water high in the air so that the dock was bathed in a continuous shower of spray. By the time it arrived in Sydney every pump and every piece of machinery on board was rusted solid. The strange part of the story was that although the condition of the dock was strikingly apparent to everyone who saw it in every port between Gibraltar and Sydney, there seemed to be no way in which this grotesque bureaucratic folly could be halted. Once started the machinery had to flog it out to the bitter end. The bitter end came in Sydney when the Australian engineers who were given the job of putting the dock in order, screamed derision and ridicule at the naval authorities, as only Australians could do. The dock was cut up for scrap iron and no more was ever heard of A.F.D. 17.

I drifted into towing more by accident than by design but I believe I was fascinated by it because it was one of the last branches of the art of sailorizing which still required all the skills of real seamanship. Handling the cable laid towing hawsers, 22 inches in circumference, on the gale-lashed after-deck of a tug like the *Integrity*, with gog lines and chain stoppers and all the paraphernalia of towing was dangerous, skilled and satisfying work. The tedium of the tow when a speed of perhaps three or four knots was achieved with the engines at full throttle for weeks on end, was always, in the end, relieved not only by the delirious joys of port but also by a sense of real achievement. I have never minded going slowly in a world which usually goes too fast.

During the early evening the swell increased—I ought to have understood the significance of it. *Iskra* towed steadily and evenly—there wasn't enough wind to switch off the engine but I determined that once we were turned on our new course I would stop it for the night even if she made poor progress. Paul and I took watches at the tiller and tried, without success, to sleep between. We were both too keyed up—too tense with the excitement of it to sleep. Tomorrow, after a night at sea, we might sleep and by tomorrow night we would be sleeping soundly and naturally in our watches below. Bill came on the radio again in the afternoon. He had put nearly a whole drum of cement into the stem and for the time being at least it was holding. He had improvised a box with wood and nails round the top of the stem inside the hull and had forced the cement in. He had almost been sick with the stench of the airless space right up in the *Integrity's* bows. Every time she dipped the water squirted at him as if from a pressure hose, splattering him with an abrasive and unpleasant brown emulsion of water and cement. But now the pump was running less, which was a relief. I was already beginning to do mental arithmetic. At the rate the pump had been going earlier in the afternoon we would soon be short of petrol. From *The Yachtsman's Guide to the Bahamas* there was only one anchorage we could possibly make with the *Integrity* in tow—Providenciales where Bamber had wanted me to go. It would be difficult and dangerous but it might be necessary to put in there for petrol.

Bill came through on the radio again just before dark and Paul, who was steering, called me up. "Bill wants to know how far north you're going—says it's cold up there—figures he'll need some warm clothes." The evening had a thick, yellow look about it—probably some local weather effect but not too healthy. I stood up in the stern with the walkie-talkie and tried to hold a conversation, with Paul translating the crackle into American. Bill was in good order—he had eaten some bread and peanut butter and made himself coffee. The cement seemed to be holding but he wasn't satisfied with it. He said he would make a stronger and bigger cement box the next day and strengthen the job. Although I couldn't understand much of what he said, his voice sounded strained and worried. I told him we had almost made our offing and said I would alter course soon towards the west. "Have a good
141

night," I told him; "if the weather keeps up and the wind freshens a little we should make good speed tomorrow." Then, for the first time, Bill's voice came through the atmospherics loud and clear and I could hear every word. He said, "Wind? Are you crazy? Man—just take a look round there—behind your back." I turned round, surprised, and looked towards the north. I believe Paul would have told me what was there if his eyes had not been glued to the compass. It was a cloud like a great diseased hand with crooked and outstretched fingers, hairy with blown wisps of black, reaching out from the horizon and spreading over the sky towards *Iskra* like an evil black mantle. Underneath it, low down on the surface of the sea, there was a smaller and blacker cloud which seemed to be making purposefully and fast towards us. I said, "Christ"—threw the walkie-talkie into the cabin and ran for the halyards.

A cloud like
a great
diseased hand.

142

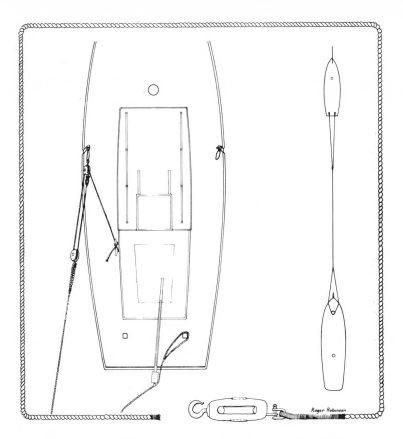

Iskra's *improvised towing arrangement worked well. It was intended to compensate for the* Integrity's *heavy drag on her stern which, without the special gear, would have prevented* Iskra *from steering properly and from making sharp turns. In* Iskra's *case the tackle had to be moved across when she changed tack because there was only one tackle on board, but the arrangement would work better with two tackles in position. The angle of the yacht to the tow line can then be adjusted as required. It was found that in a light or moderate wind on the beam she tended to luff, so that it was necessary to haul in on the tackle. When hit by a heavy squall from well before the beam she became unmanageable and bore away until she was broadside on to the tow—a position of danger for any towing vessel.*

143

CHAPTER XIV

There is a feeling of dryness in the mouth, a tightening of muscles in the throat, a drawing away of blood, a sensation that the skin is shrinking over the head. The feeling comes with a sudden fear. It is the stronger when you understand that the predicament is of your own making and stronger again when other people are involved for whom you must be responsible. At first the feeling paralyses, renders the mind and the body inert and incapable of thought or action. Then the senses and the physical responses come crowding back and like a boxer recovering from a knock-out, blood rushes back to the drained spaces of the brain, bringing with it the will and the ability to act. I stood in *Iskra's* cockpit for no more than an instant, looking through the starlit night at Paul, at the familiar shapes and forms of the boat, at the dark bulk of the *Integrity*—seeing nothing. Then I was released.

As I leapt for the halyards and reef pendants the stars blacked out. The cloud clamped over like an iron lid. The wind switched from east to north and came at us with a vicious and truculent whine, driving hard, stinging drops of rain horizontally into our faces. Caught aback, *Iskra* trembled in the wind's eye, the sails shaking with such violence that she staggered. "Stays'l sheet", I yelled at Paul through the frenzy

145

of noise. "Pull it in—tight—starboard side." Somehow he knew what to do—by instinct or by acute observation since he had been on board. As I dropped the mainsail to the third reef the staysail filled and *Iskra's* bow paid off. The flapping and shaking stopped suddenly as the sails took the wind. I tied in the reef cringles as she heeled to the squall. Pinned to the *Integrity* by her stern she was lifeless and unmanageable. She heeled over to port, forced over by a sudden gust of extra strength within the squall. Leaving the halyards in a heap I ran across the crazily sloping deck to the cockpit. Paul was still concentrating his mind on the compass—it was the only thing he knew in this sudden bedlam. I gave him the tripping line for the jib furling. "Pull—steadily and hard." I eased the straining sheet and the jib rolled away. *Iskra* was still going over—she had put her side-decks under, the water was creeping up towards the cockpit. The tiller was hard over but she couldn't answer. Something would have to give or she would go under—she was slowly turning off the wind and I could do nothing to stop her. She was like a dog fastened by a chain, the fire creeping up.

Paul said, "It's the tow line holding her." I looked for the *Integrity*. I could see nothing through the blackness and the driving rain. Paul made out her dark shape almost on our beam to leeward and pointed his arm. *Iskra* had turned through a right angle. The weight of the *Integrity* with the windage on her high hull was pulling *Iskra* sideways—added to the sheer pressure of the wind it was pulling her over, a classic situation of danger for a vessel towing. The tackle was her only chance. It was ready to hand. I hooked it on to the strop I had made ready on the starboard side, and the hauling part to the towing bridle. As I sat on the side decks, braced my feet against the cockpit coaming and took the strain I could see the water already lapping the lee side. The tiller swung limp and useless. The end of the boom and the bottom of the sail were dragging in the sea—the carelessly reefed mainsail was shaking up the leach, shaking the mast, shaking the whole boat as she lay trembling on her beam

146

Her dark shape almost on our beam to leeward.

ends—trembling as if in mortal fear for her life. Paul was standing now with his feet on the cockpit side holding to the opposite coaming. "Let go the bridle Paul—quick for Christ's sake." He looked at me, uncomprehending. "Down there— the bridle—pull it off the samson post—quick." The angle of heel and the direction of the tow line would help him—if he could only pull the eye upwards two or three inches it would slip off. I saw him bend down and grasp the rope—it was already under water. Then he turned and looked at me for confirmation. "Let it go man—let it go—pull it off the post." I saw him arch his back and pull. At first it wouldn't shift—it was bar tight with strain. Now the sea was pouring into the cockpit. "Pull man—for Jesus' sake pull." He put his right foot over the coaming and into the lee scuppers—up to the knee in water. Then he bent over the rope and pulled with all his might.

The bridle slipped off the oak post with a thud which

147

Now the sea was pouring into the cockpit.

shook the boat through to her keel bolts and the rope flew out of Paul's hands. She sprang up as if released from some over-powering weight. Paul lost his balance and tumbled headlong into the cockpit, his fall broken by water which was up to the coaming. As she came up she deluged him with a cascade of sea falling down from the sail. I was almost thrown over-board off the weather side deck as she righted herself—I grabbed for the handrail along the coach roof. I eased the tackle to the bitter end as the strain came on it to give *Iskra* a chance to recover herself. The seas had built up quickly and were slapping against the weather side and sending spray stinging across the boat. As I heaved again on the tackle she slowly came round and slowly gathered her way. Paul recovered himself quickly and stood at the tiller. Now with the weight of the tow shifted away from the stern she would steer—I gave Paul a course which made her as comfortable as possible with the *Integrity* lying off her lee quarter and the wind

148

broad on the bow. The first fierceness of the squall was spent—the rain stopped and the wind steadied and eased slightly. Now it was blowing an easy Force 6 but the sea was increasing with every minute, white crests showing through the night with dim phosphorescent pallor. *Iskra* was pitching into them more than she would have done without the *Integrity* astern and sometimes they would roll green over the foredeck. We hadn't given a thought to the *Integrity* or to Bill—they would have to wait. We didn't know whether the pump was running. Nothing could be heard over the sonorous whine of the wind and the hissing sea.

Nothing had carried away, nothing was broken—the engine was still turning over steadily at slow revs. I tried switching it off and to my satisfaction I found that she would still steer without it—it seemed quiet and was a relief when it was stopped. With three reefs, the staysail and the jib rolled up *Iskra* was steady. I tidied the mainsail which had never been properly reefed, tying in the points and shaking out the water that was trapped in the folds of the sail. I coiled the halyards and stowed them on their pins round the mast, pumped the bilge—there was a good deal of water in it—checked the rigging and found everything sound. The leg of the bridle that Paul had let go was still in the water. It could stay there for the time being—we would get it back when things quietened down. Below, the shambles was not as bad as I had feared. A few things had taken flight from the starboard side to the port side—there was a broken plate and the contents of the cutlery box had been spread along the lee bunk. The walkie-talkie was where I had thrown it and was unharmed. Thank the Lord we had sea room. She would be making leeway now and would be driving steadily towards the coast but she should be safe until daylight. I took a bearing of the loom of the light on the north end of Turks which was all I could see. The light on Cape Comete—the north point of Caicos which would have shown the position of the Phillips Reef, was not to be seen. I guessed it wasn't working—the guide to the Bahamas marked it as unreliable. It was uncomfortable and unpleasant but it was bearable and perhaps it wouldn't last for long. If it was a typical norther it would be over inside a few hours. I changed into dry clothes and relieved Paul while he did the same. Then Paul took the helm again and I went below to prepare a hot meal. I was searching in the locker for soup when Paul said, "Hey—Frank—she won't steer—the sail's flapping."

I could see at once that something was wrong but not at once what it was. *Iskra* had slowed down although the wind was as strong. The tiller was hard a-weather but she wouldn't answer and she was coming closer and closer to the wind. Soon she would be in irons. I started the engine again and let it turn at slow revs and then I looked astern and saw that

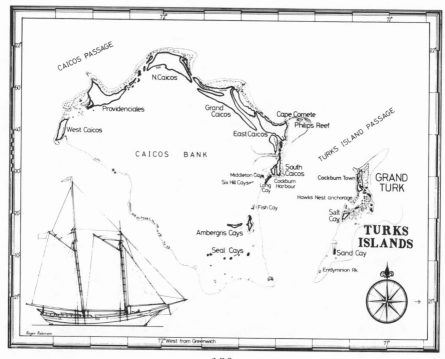

the *Integrity* was lying right out on the quarter. Through the binoculars it seemed as if she was lying more across the wind—I could see the whole length of her instead of only the bow. She was pulling *Iskra* round and whatever I did to the tackle wouldn't stop it. I put my hand inside the cabin, reached the torch and began to flash the *Integrity* while Paul listened on the radio. Nothing came through. Then I went inside the cabin and fetched out a white flare, tore the top off it and rubbed the abrasive surfaces together. The flare spluttered alight and as I held it above my head the whiteness shone round with blinding clarity so that every detail of *Iskra* and of the wild seascape was thrown into stark relief. I waved it back and forth and then threw it high in the air so that it made an arc of light with the last of its force before it fell with a brief splutter into the sea. Paul and I waited for more minutes, not exchanging a word but each of us consumed by our anxiety. I was in the cabin fetching another flare when Bill came crackling through. "Listen you guys—I got problems—the tiller's broken off the rudder head—the helm's jammed hard over to port—I can't shift it. Just leave it with me—I'll come back to you", and he went off the air without waiting for our reply.

Paul and I got back the other leg of the bridle. We hauled tight on the tackle until the shackle was within reach and then Paul stretched himself out over the stern, grabbed the slack rope and brought the eye inboard. We moved the tackle across and managed to get *Iskra* to steer again but now the *Integrity* was lying almost broadside on to the seas and we could hardly move her. It was like pulling against a ring bolt on the dock—she just didn't move. *Iskra* was pitching violently, water was rolling over the bow and crashing against the fore part of the cabin top. She was beginning to be punished and I didn't like it. It didn't seem to make any difference if the engine was running or not except that when it was running it raced and vibrated violently when *Iskra's* head went under. I switched it off. Now the wind was taking us to leeward much more quickly. I could see from my compass bearings of the

151

light on Turks that we were driving down on Phillips Reef—an ugly outcrop of coral three miles to seaward of Cape Comete. There was no way of telling from a single bearing whether the reef was directly under our lee or whether we would pass clear of it. Better to take no chances. "We'll give Bill another half hour and if he doesn't fix it we'll put her about and haul off shore—or at least we'll try." It wouldn't be easy to get her through stays in this wind with the *Integrity* now a dead weight. I didn't know whether Paul understood or whether he was baffled by the whole strange performance. His baptism to sailing was a traumatic one. The wind had freshened again. Pinned down by the tow and without her ability to weave and swerve and dodge, *Iskra* was taking heavy water on board—an element of discomfort added to the anxiety. Then we saw Bill flashing.

With Paul's help I could make out his voice through the crackle. "There's no way I can fix that tiller—it's just jammed on the top of the rudder with nails man—they just bent over and it came off. I hammered it on again with some more nails—it just broke off again. It's jammed over solid—I guess the goddam thing's broken underneath. Listen Frank—for Jesus' sake—what do we want the fucking tiller for? This packet's sinking man—fast. The pump's been running two hours an' it's still coming up. I just went below with a torch man—the bow's like Niagara. The planks are all broken open an' the sea's just comin' in real fine. The cement's all gone—man there's no sign of it—she's washed clean. If this hooker doesn't sink inside an hour I'll shit bricks man. You just tell me what to do next—maybe Bamber knows." I thought for a moment on this news—it required proper consideration. "Tell him I'll call him back inside five minutes," I said to Paul.

I looked again at the chart and took another bearing of Turks—it was no more than a finger of light now, swinging across the low cloud once every ten seconds. If we turned back we would have the wind behind us, at least once we got back into the Turks Islands Passage. There was no way of telling how far we would have to go before we had the clear water of the passage under our lee unless the light on Cape Comete came on. I calculated our speed and courses as best I could and made a guess at the drift to leeward. I doubted whether we had more than five miles between us and the Phillips Reef now—in this wind she would drift that distance in a couple of hours—and it might be even closer. With the *Integrity's* rudder jammed over our chances of holding her off were small. Again, if she was leaking as much as Bill said, we would never keep her afloat even until daylight, let alone all the way back to the anchorage at Turks. Even if we did get her back to Turk—what then? She would have to be taken back to the Hawk's Nest anchorage and beached. At the best it would take six hours. If Bill could get the spare pump working as well—improvise another suction hose out of the existing discharge hose—it might be possible. I flashed Bill with the torch and he came on the radio at once. "Listen Bill— how long will she stay afloat?" "Not much more than an hour and a half—maybe an hour. It's over the lockers already. She's beginning to wallow." "Suppose you could get the other pump working as well?" "No way man—I'm using it already. The first one broke down—seized up—something jammed in the piston."

Now it was final and decisive—there was no room for choice. The *Integrity* would wait no longer, she had come to the end and she would not turn back. "Okay Bill—we'll take you off. I'll shorten up the tow and bring you across on the float—but first I'll put her over on the other tack. We're getting close to the reef." I knew it would be difficult and it might take a long time to get Bill off. Besides, if there was a chance, I would like to get some of my gear back. On the other tack the *Integrity,* with her damaged rudder, would lie head to wind instead of broadside on and would make half the leeway. She would roll less and she would probably leak less.

I was getting used to the complications of putting *Iskra* through stays with the *Integrity* in tow. Paul and I had the routine well practised now and we could do it without a

153

mistake—I thought. This time it would be more difficult because the wind was stronger, it was rougher and there was more strain on the tow. I started up the engine again and gave her full throttle. Paul steered and I eased the tackle enough to put the eye of the bridle over the samson post on the lee side. *Iskra* was heeling hard to port. Every time a big sea came over it swept aft, flooding the side decks and tumbling over the cabin top. I unhooked the tackle from the lee bridle and the strop, carried it across to the weather side quickly before *Iskra* could be blown to leeward and hooked it to the strop and the eye of the weather bridle. Then I braced myself on the side decks with my feet against the coaming and hove the tackle tight. "Let her come Paul," I shouted; "hard over." He put the helm down and as *Iskra* came into the wind I helped her round with the tackle.

When she was truly in stays, the mainsail and the staysail flapping wildly and the way off her, she was picked up by a wave which was out of all proportion to those that had gone before it. I remember that I turned half round as I felt her lift, saw behind me a concave wall of black water, its tottering crest high above me, unstable and already turning in on itself, drawing in its great breath for the final explosion of its pent-up power. I remember noticing that the eye of the lee bridle floated clear of the samson post as the water came on deck, remember making a mental note that once she was round we would have to retrieve it. Then the world seemed to come to pieces around me. I saw Paul let go the tiller and grab for the life lines round the cockpit as the explosion grew in strength. I looked up and saw it descending. There was a crash and then there was rushing water everywhere—wrenching and pulling at me and striving to tear me free. I must have let go the hauling part of the tackle and grabbed the handrail on the cabin top with both hands. The water seemed to be falling vertically—seemed to be a solid substance that pummelled and battered and flattened me to the deck. The only thought that was in my mind was that I should hang on— hold tight to what I was grasping with a blind, unquestioning

154

instinct. I don't know how I held on. It seemed to go on for a long time, this tearing and pulling and this deafening noise and this avalanche of water. Then I seemed to come to the surface. Seemed to be able to breathe and see. I heard the beat of the engine and felt its vibrations. I looked for Paul and saw him still standing in the cockpit, the water up to his waist, still grasping the life lines as I was still grasping the handrail. He was trying to say something. His lips moved when he saw me but I couldn't hear his words. The engine was racing, the sea seemed to be rushing past my body as I lay stretched on the side decks. *Iskra* was heeling over, her movement had changed—she seemed to be rushing through the waves as she used to do. I dragged myself up and tumbled into the water-logged cockpit beside Paul, automatically put my hand inside the cabin to the switchboard and turned off the engine. When it stopped there was a moment of blessed quiet. I turned to Paul. "What?" I said. He looked at me with horror in his eyes, "The *Integrity*," he said, "the *Integrity*— she's gone."

CHAPTER XV

At first, Paul's words had no effect on me. I heard what he said but the information made no impact. I may have been slightly shocked—I remember a feeling of joy and satisfaction that *Iskra* was at last sailing as she ought to sail. She seemed to be flying after the hours of slog, swerving and side-stepping with all her old agility and grace, flirting with the waves, sometimes taking a white crest and flinging it defiantly across the deck, feinting, dodging, parrying. She was carrying the right amount of sail. It was blowing hard but not more than she could manage—the seas were big but nothing to worry her now that she was free. I knew that it was only because she had been tied up and helpless that she had been overwhelmed. There was a fair lot of water in her. I saw it slopping over the cabin sole and instinctively my hand went to the pump. Then I saw the strop for the tackle on the starboard side—the hook was still fast to it. The tackle had run free leaving the bare end trailing in the sea. Now, looking back, I wonder whether it was only carelessness that had left the knot unmade—there may have been a significance in it. Perhaps some force inside me had ordained it. I remember it had come into my head two or three times during those days of preparation that I must put a stop-knot in the end of the tackle to prevent the rope from

157

running out through the blocks. Somehow it was never done. I heard Paul say, impatiently, "Well, come on man, what are you going to do about it?" I came to my senses.

The night was black—there was nothing to be seen outside the narrow radius of our vision—no stars, no horizon not even the light on Turks. There was no sign whatever of the *Integrity*. She would be careering downwind with no restraint and with half a gale behind her. It was no more than a guess whether she would be driven ashore on the reef or whether she would sink first—either way Bill was in dire peril. He had the float but in these conditions there was no telling how he would survive on it. Amidst the fury of the reef his chances were nil. Either way, the reef or the bottom, we had an hour to find him.

After she had recovered herself and had shaken herself free of the great weight of water, *Iskra* had fallen off on the port tack. Now she was sailing across the Turks Islands Passage at six knots, I guessed, on an easterly course with the wind fine before the beam. I looked in at the clock and noted the time. Noted the compass course. "We'll put her about", I said to Paul, "Lee ho!" She came flying into the wind and payed off easily on the other tack.

I did not know whether the same course had been maintained accurately since we lost the *Integrity*—did not know the exact number of minutes that had elapsed, did not know the rate of the *Integrity's* drift, could only guess at our own speed and leeway. On the reciprocal course *Iskra* had the wind slightly abaft the beam and she was going faster. I guessed we couldn't have been sailing away from the *Integrity* for more than ten minutes but we would have covered a mile in that time. We sailed back for a quarter of an hour and there was no sign of her—nothing more than the black sea and the impersonal breaking waves with their momentary flashes of luminous white. I had allowed ten degrees for our own leeway and the *Integrity's* drift. Perhaps it was too much—or not enough? Paul and I gazed into the night and the night threw our stare back in our faces. We put about again and

158

surged across the other way, now luffing a fraction in case I had allowed too much. Five minutes this time and then about again and more down wind. Christ, we must have got too far down wind—haul the sheets and make three short tacks close hauled. In half an hour we criss-crossed the ocean with a pattern of lines which lost all reason and all logic. We were ourselves lost—lurching back and forth across the Turks Islands Passage blindly, hopelessly, searching through the blackness, peering into the opaque walls which oppressed us and served to deaden our senses—the lost searching for the lost. Paul listened on the radio, holding it in his hand and talking at it as if he could conjure Bill out of the night with its magic. But I knew, we both knew, that its range was measured in yards. It had started to rain heavily and the wind had eased—the norther going through I guessed—it would be fine in a couple of hours, or less. Now I could hear the reef—oh Jesus—that uncompromising, low rumble, still faint but gaining in strength. We must be too far to the west—"Lee ho!" Now it was a mindless, aimless, and thoughtless zig-zag—an erratic darting from side to side without hope and without system. We lit our white flares until we only had one left. They blinded us so that we could see nothing through their brightness. I put about again with a sick, hopeless feeling of disaster and tragedy inside me. How could this ever be justified to myself, to anyone? There was no way in which blame could be denied or excused. A mere detail had brought disaster—as happens at sea. I had learnt the lesson a hundred times and still I was ignorant of it. In seamanship every fragment of preparation is as important as every other—the big and the small are all as equals—every part interlocks with every other. A simple figure of eight knot in the bitter end of a tackle was left undone—the tackle ran through the blocks, the tow, with Bill on board, was lost. There wasn't much time left. I glanced in at the clock—we had been searching for the *Integrity* for forty minutes—by now she would be near to sinking. Bill would be getting ready to leave her in the float, preparing himself for a journey which might be his last. I felt

sick with apprehension—at best he would drift through the
night to be picked up tomorrow or to be cast ashore on some
deserted beach in North Caicos. At worst there was the reef.
All this travail, all this expenditure of thought and effort and
resources, culminating in failure and possibly in tragedy, for
the sake of a worthless basket of rotten wood and sick nails.
The guilt of it would hang round me for ever.

I didn't know what shortcoming it was in us—arrogance
perhaps or over-confidence or too glib an assumption of the
sea's good will—that had singled us out for this treatment.
Suffice it that we were spared the ultimate price—forgiven the
last penalty. The ocean is mysterious in its dispositions. Bill's
last white flare burst into the night immediately ahead of us,
flooding the *Integrity* and *Iskra* and a tight ring of the sea
with a harsh, metallic brilliance as if we had been momentarily

*Bill's last white flare burst into the
night immediately ahead of us.*

160

caught in the beam of a searchlight. The schooner was no more than a couple of boats lengths from the bowsprit end—I put the helm hard down before *Iskra* ran full tilt into her. We looked at Bill and he at us in astonishment as we sheered alongside within feet of him. "I thought you guys had gone home," he shouted, "I guess you'd better be quick." We could see every detail of the *Integrity's* deck as Bill held the flare high above his head. The pump was still running and the water still tumbled out through the scuppers but now, instead of riding high and rolling in the seas, she was still in the water, low like a fully loaded barge and the waves were washing over her decks as if she was fastened to the bottom. She had the look of doom about her—there was no saving her now. I felt a profound relief which flooded through my body—a great happiness and a lightening of the spirit. The *Integrity* had never done harm to any person and in this she had remained true. She had met with adversity, she had suffered and she bore the scars of her misfortunes but she had never hurt any man—had never struck against those who had been associated with her. I glanced at Paul as *Iskra* came into the wind—the tears were rolling down his cheeks.

As *Iskra* passed close to the *Integrity* I yelled, "Show us a light Bill and keep it burning." I said to Paul, "Watch the *Integrity*—don't do anything else—just watch her—don't take your eyes off her." Before I left the cockpit I took a rough bearing. "East by north Paul—remember that." By the time I got the halyards free *Iskra* had already payed off on the other tack and was making away from the *Integrity*. The rain was coming down solid—thick and heavy, cutting visibility to yards. As I clawed down the sails the flare went out and our world was in darkness again. Paul shouted, "I can't see her but I've got the bearing." "Just keep looking." It seemed to take an age to get the sails down, the main sheet hauled tight, the boom into the gallows, the swinging gaff secured and the heavy and stiff folds of the sail lashed with tyers. I had done it a thousand times but now every piece of gear I touched seemed stricken with perversity—knots came

161

undone, ropes slipped out of my hands, loose coils caught round my feet, I tripped and blundered in the dark as if I had never been aboard a boat before. As soon as the mainsail and the staysail were off her she rolled abominably in the swell and the remains of the sea. The rumble of the reef was louder and more sinister. I started the engine and put her slow ahead on east by north—080° near enough. Paul and I strained our eyes through the rain. Surely we couldn't lose her now—it wasn't possible—we must be within yards. Then we heard the noise of the pump and saw a light ahead and to windward—a piece of rag or a shirt soaked in paraffin I guessed, hung on the *Integrity's* stump. It burnt with an eerie, yellow light, spluttering in the rain, a thick smoke streaming away from it.

As we got closer Paul started the radio and we flashed Bill with a torch. "Tell him we'll come alongside, Paul—tell him to jump as we come past." It wouldn't be easy to bring her close the way *Iskra* was pitching and rolling. It might have been better under sail when she would have been steadier. Paul said, "Bill says to make fast—he's gonna transfer gear over. Says he's okay for ten minutes." I put the engine in neutral and went below to find a rope—sorted through the gear in the fo'c'sle for a mooring line I knew was there—an old piece of sisal I used for odd jobs—it was well worn and easy to coil. I was shaking—there couldn't be much time left. Christ, that man had some nerve. It was in my mind to tell him to leave the gear but—well, there was no denying it would be good to get some of it back. I found the line in front of my eyes when I had been searching for five minutes. I felt claustrophobic in the fo'c'sle—time was slipping away and I was below blinding myself with light, panic building up dangerously inside me. *Iskra* had drifted away and turned off the wind when I got back to the cockpit but we could still see the yellow smudge of light from the *Integrity's* mast. I put her in gear, speeded up the engine and pulled the tiller hard over. She rolled her rails under as she came round. I gave Paul the coil of rope. "Get up on the side decks, port side, throw it when I tell you—not before." I would have to get close—I doubted whether Paul knew the correct way to throw a rope. *Iskra* was head to the seas, pitching violently, difficult to steer without much way on her.

As she came close to the *Integrity's* stern the two yachts seemed to be leaping up and down like pistons—one second I looked down on the *Integrity's* deck—saw Bill's thin, lanky, loose-limbed form surrounded by carefully heaped piles of *Iskra's* gear. He had been busy while the *Integrity* was lost—maybe he had occupied himself to keep himself from thinking of his plight. He had collected everything that was on board and he had made neat mounds, ready for passing over to *Iskra*. The float was in the water, tied to the *Integrity's* stern to port leaving the starboard side, where there was some lee, free for *Iskra*. Bill was a born seaman. He knew how to use his brain, how to think ahead. As *Iskra* dropped into the trough and the *Integrity* rose, I could see under her scarred and jagged counter, could see the top of the rudder as it came clear of the waves still jammed over to port. One blow from that counter would splinter *Iskra* wide open—one false step, a sudden and unpredicted sea drawing the yachts together, would shatter *Iskra* as the *Integrity* herself had been shattered by the *Bela Krajina's* stern. I came as close as I dared. Paul was standing on the side deck braced against the life line, striving to keep balance and holding the coil of rope in his hand. "Right—heave it over." Bill was leaning over the *Integrity's* rail ready to receive the line. I saw Paul draw his arm back, holding all the coil in his left hand and the end of the rope in his right hand. The coil was too bulky, it should have been split into two—*Iskra* was so close that it must reach. As he threw the coil caught on *Iskra's* life line. It seemed to explode in the air, the end flew bravely towards Bill—he stretched his long body out over the *Integrity's* rail but the bare end failed to reach him. It came to within an inch of his grasping fingers and then it drew back and fell with the coil into the sea. There is nothing so ignominious and humiliating as a heaving line that fails. I cursed—Paul looked hurt and helpless. I put the helm over to

163

make another turn and try again. The rope caught round *Iskra's* propeller and the engine stopped dead.

When things begin to go wrong at sea they seldom confine themselves to a single malicious stroke—rather they launch themselves into a cycle of misfortunes which, feeding upon themselves, escalate and pile on one setback over another until a degree of wretchedness is reached which in some way causes the cycle to turn the other way—perhaps, in the end, misfortune reaches a natural point of saturation. So it happened with Paul and me and the *Integrity*. We were still within twenty feet of her, still pitching up and down beside her when the engine cut. I saw Bill feverishly looking for a rope or any piece of anything that could bridge that small but widening gap. I looked round *Iskra's* deck, at a loss. By the time I got to the fo'c'sle, found a line and brought it back, I knew the *Integrity* would be far out of reach and probably far out of sight. My brain seemed to have been paralyzed by the rapid rise and fall of the emotional temperature over the last hour and was now spent and incapable of constructive thought. I knew we would have to set sail on *Iskra* again— would have to go through the reverse process of setting the mainsail, the staysail and the jib and then beat back through the rain, find the *Integrity* again and somehow take Bill off under sail. I wondered whether the *Integrity* could possibly stay afloat for long enough. It might take half an hour. The whole business seemed too difficult to undertake— seemed doomed to failure before it started.

It was Paul who was responsible for causing the cycle to change direction in our favour. I believe it was by an intuitive and happy instinct. Being unfamiliar with the whole environment in which he found himself, his mind was able to perceive simplicity where my own was bogged down by complications. By an act of plain common sense he cut through the at once confused and disheartened processes of my own thinking. He picked up the coil of *Iskra's* main sheet which was lying neatly on the side deck at his feet and without waiting for instruction, threw it underarm at the *Integrity*.

164

The rope flew across the space between the two yachts and the end cleverly wound itself round one of the *Integrity's* wooden stanchions. Bill had turned away and didn't see it. We both yelled at him in unison, "There it is man—quick—round the stanchion." We saw him look through the dark, puzzled, as the rope drew tight and then just before it must unwind itself and drop back into the sea, he saw it, grasped it and pulled. *Iskra's* stern came round towards the *Integrity* as Bill shortened in and her bow paid off downwind. "All fast," Bill shouted across.

Now Bill became a dynamo of activity. He had been waiting for and planning for this moment ever since it had been decided to abandon the *Integrity* and he was determined not to miss it. He took no notice when I shouted, "Leave the gear Bill—come yourself and leave it." The *Integrity* must be in her last throes. She was lurching and wallowing now, the sea washing freely over her 'midships section. She looked unstable, as if at any second she might roll and not recover, roll over on her beam ends or plunge her stern and slide to the bottom. Bill knew what he was doing and he worked fast. He moved the float round and tied it between *Iskra* and the *Integrity*, shortening up until it exactly filled the space between the two yachts. To stop *Iskra* from falling back against it I broke out her roller jib. We got the main sheet back, changing it for an odd rope Bill found in the *Integrity's* bow. Bill started passing the gear over to us, using the float as a bridge. He would jump down into it with incredible agility, a pile of gear in his arms, stagger across it somehow balancing himself against the motion and pass the gear to Paul who leaned himself over *Iskra's* stern. Paul passed it to me and I took it below and piled it on the cabin sole and in the fo'c'sle. I saw my beloved primus stove, still in its gimbal, come home—the kettle witness to a thousand scrapes come back to its own quarters—boxes full of tins, water cans, the sails I had put on board, tools, cutlery, Chauncey's walkie-talkie—every single thing I had put on board the *Integrity* came back except what had been consumed. Bill's priorities were unswerving. Down to the jar of peanut butter, sorely dented by this time and the *Pilgrim's Progress* I got all *Iskra's* gear back. I believe he regarded his first loyalty as mine and it was not until everything of mine had been returned that he switched his attention to what was left.

The *Integrity* was going fast. Bill wanted to get the motor pump—the one that was not in use. "Leave it man—come yourself—what the hell does it matter?" I shouted at him. He wouldn't listen. He was humping the heavy pump across the *Integrity's* deck when she gave a lurch to starboard. "Bill— for Jesus sake—do as I tell you—come on board—she's going." I saw him look round and then by a miraculous feat of strength and balance he got the pump jammed across the *Integrity's* rail—he vaulted over into the float and then he pulled the pump in after him. Caught off balance by a sudden lurch with the heavy pump in his hands he half tumbled on to the bulbous side of the float. The pump fell in front of him. There was a faint crack like a pistol shot heard from a great distance and a loud hiss of escaping air. As we watched, the float collapsed inwards on itself—suddenly lost its form and disappeared bubbling and spluttering, dragged under by the weight of the pump. Bill was left floundering in the sea between *Iskra* and the *Integrity*. Paul leaned over *Iskra's* side grasped an arm, I grasped the other and we both pulled upwards—Bill came up over the rail, his long form attenuated and streaming water like some bizarre sea monster. "Jesus," he said, "I could do with a drink."

Paul gave him a glass of rum and he squatted down on the cockpit floor from where he could see the *Integrity*. The wind had eased again—it wasn't much more than Force 5 now—the rain stopped and a pale star shone through the scudding cloud. I was anxious to cut and leave the *Integrity*—she might sink within minutes and I didn't want to be tied to her when she took the final plunge. Bill wanted to stay and watch her go down, "I want to see that bastard sink," he said bitterly, "so's I know goddam well she can't come back." We waited for five minutes. Bill had another glass of rum. The thunder

166

Bill came up over the rail, his long form attenuated and streaming water like some bizarre sea monster.

of the reef grew stronger and nearer. We heard the motor pump cough and splutter and die. "Out of gas," Bill said. There was a sudden peace—I felt pleased that the *Integrity* should live through her last minutes in silence. I felt unwilling to stay and watch her die—she should be allowed the consideration of privacy for her last act. She had been mocked by death often enough over the years—now she should be allowed to meet it alone and in her own way. She looked somehow grotesque and squalid in her agony, the stump of her mast like a decayed old tooth, the sea already embracing her. The stench of decay still wafted down to us. She was like an exhumed corpse, buried twice already, disturbed twice from her peace and now forced yet again to live through the indignity of death. Well she should do it in as much peace as it was in my power to give her—after this there would be no further humiliation. Bill's head was already nodding—exhaustion and the drink had done for him. Paul was in the cabin. I glanced down, he had fallen asleep sitting on the starboard bunk hunched in discomfort. The strain and unfamiliar exertions and excitements of the day and the night had been enough for him. He had carried them well.

I took out my knife and stood over the rope. I looked at the *Integrity* for the last time and it seemed to me that I saw her not as she was but as she had been—the pride of the coast, the schooner of Waldo's dream, the finest creation that Captain Culler's cunning and artistry had ever conceived. I saw her with her tan-barked sails and her bottle green hull pacing the seas with a bone in her mouth, heeling to the breeze, queening it over the ocean, full of grace and pride and good breeding. I saw her in her glory—a thing of beauty, strong and fleet and dignified, holding her head high, every man's pride, a bringer of joy to every heart. I raised the knife and struck at the rope—the strands flew apart. I kept my head down for a moment watching the water under *Iskra's* stern as she gathered her way. Now that the *Integrity* was gone life would gradually slot back into its old groove, I would find myself able to take up again what I had put to one side. I would land Bill and Paul in Turks, complete the voyage to Nassau as quickly as possible—if I hurried I would be there in time. Tamarind's birthday was, after all, an important occasion— no one has a first birthday more than once. I found that I wanted to see her with a deep longing. After the weeks and months of solitude I needed to love and be loved or I would become detached and desiccated, my being warped by loneliness. I felt a profound relief now that the *Integrity* had gone to her proper and natural place where no hand could ever disturb her again. She would make her leisurely way to the bottom nearly two thousand fathoms down. She would glide through the cool waters meandering gracefully downwards in oblique curves towards the sea bed. She would scan the dark floor of the ocean and find for herself some coral bower softly cushioned with the deep's fantastic vegetation where she would while away her final retirement, safe forever from greed and duplicity. I was pleased that she had gone—

pleased for her, pleased for Waldo and Captain Culler, pleased for everyone who had loved her and pleased for myself. "Good luck you poor bastard," I said, "it will be better for you where you are going."

When I looked up the *Integrity* was gone—swallowed into the night, cradled for ever within the ocean's bosom.